Family Emergency Preparedness Manual

By members of:

THE CHURCH OF
JESUS CHRIST
OF LATTER-DAY SAINTS

Contents

- **EMERGENCY BASICS** ... 1
  - BEFORE AN EMERGENCY ... 1
  - DURING AN EMERGENCY ... 3
  - AFTER AN EMERGENCY ... 4
- **IN CASE OF:** ... 5
  - EARTHQUAKE ... 5
    - BEFORE: ... 5
    - DURING: ... 5
    - AFTER: ... 6
  - POWER OUTAGE ... 7
    - BEFORE: ... 7
    - DURING: ... 7
    - AFTER: ... 8
  - HIGH WINDS ... 9
    - BEFORE: ... 9
    - DURING: ... 9
    - AFTER: ... 9
  - SEVERE THUNDER & LIGHTNING ... 10
    - INDOORS: ... 10
    - OUTDOORS: ... 10
    - FIRST AID: ... 10
  - BLIZZARDS ... 11
  - FLOODS ... 12
    - BEFORE: ... 12
    - DURING: ... 12
    - AFTER: ... 13
  - FIRES ... 14
    - PREVENTION ... 14
    - BASIC FIREFIGHTING ... 14
    - TYPES OF FIRES ... 15
  - CHEMICAL SPILL ... 16
    - ON THE SCENE: ... 16
    - NOTIFICATION: ... 16
    - EVACUATE ... 17
    - SHELTER-IN-PLACE ... 18
- **72 HOUR EMERGENCY KIT** ... 19
  - Container ... 20
  - Water ... 20
  - Food ... 20
  - Shelter ... 21
  - Bedding ... 21
  - Clothing ... 21
  - Fuel ... 22
  - First Aid Kit ... 24
  - Miscellaneous ... 25
  - Family Information Record ... 26
  - Infants ... 27
  - Car Mini-Survival Kit ... 27
  - At-Work Survival Kit ... 27
  - Notes ... 27
- **FIRST AID BASICS** ... 28
  - Emergency Care ... 29

Immediate Lifesaving Measures	30
Communicable Disease / Pandemic	**31**
How to protect your Family	32
How the flu is spread	32
Personal Hygiene Basics	33
How to Wash Hands	33
Other Hand Cleaning Options	34
Cough and Sneeze Etiquette	35
Preparing for a Pandemic Influenza Outbreak	36
Protecting the Family – Building a Safe Haven	36
Instructions for Parents	36
Instructions for Children	36
Protecting the Individual	37
Protecting the Community	37
Public Utilities in an Emergency	**38**
Gas	38
Sewer	39
Electricity	40
Fire Safety	**41**
Getting Prepared	41
In case of Fire	42
After a Fire	42
Self Reliance	**43**
Home Storage	44
Personal and Family Finances	46
Physical Health	48
Gardening for Self Reliance	**50**
Planning a Garden	50
WHERE SHOULD I PLANT MY GARDEN?	51
HOW BIG SHOULD MY GARDEN BE?	51
HOW SHOULD I ARRANGE MY PLANTING AREA?	52
WHAT SHOULD I PLANT?	53
WHEN SHOULD I PLANT?	54
WHAT TOOLS DO I NEED?	55
HOW SHOULD I PLAN MY TIME?	56
HOW DO I PREPARE MY GARDEN?	56
HELPFUL TIPS ABOUT PLANTS AND WATER	56
WHAT IS THE EXPECTED YIELD?	57
Short Term Food Storage for the Home	**58**
Storage of Prepackaged Groceries	59
ESTIMATED SHELF LIFE OF COMERCIALLY PACKAGED FOODS	60
Long Term Food Storage for the Home	**62**
BARE-MINIMUM	62
Packaging Recommendations	64
PETE Bottles for Longer-Term Storage	70
Wheat Grinder Basics	76
Stone Grinders	76
Burr Grinders	77
Impact Grinders	77
Popular Wheat Grinders	78
Some delicious wheat recipes	81
Water Storage	**83**
Principles of Water Storage	83
Problems of water storage	83

- Practices of water storage 84
  - 55 gallon water drums 85
  - 5 gallon boxes 85
  - 250+ gallon water tanks 86
  - 1 gallon jug 87
  - Hard plastic water jugs 87
  - 4.2 ounce water pouch 88
  - PURIFICATION 89
    - Bleach 89
    - Iodine (drops/tablets) 90
    - SODIS (Solar Disinfection) 91
    - Gravity carbon filters 91
    - Chlorine 92
    - Boiling 92
    - Sports bottle with filter 93
- Important non-food items for storage 94
  - Tools 94
  - Cooking 94
  - Bedding 95
  - Clothing 95
  - Safety Items 95
  - Sanitation 96
  - Hygiene Supplies 96
  - Pets 97
- Financial Preparedness 98
- Important and Precious Documents 101
  - Family Information Record 101
- Emergency Heat 104
  - ALTERNATIVE HEAT, LIGHT, & POWER SOURCES 107
- Emergency Shelter 110
  - What You Need 110
- Driving in an Emergency 112
  - Flood 112
  - Hurricane 112
  - Tornado 112
  - Blizzard 113
  - Earthquake 113
  - Summer Heat 113
  - Developing Emergency 113
- Dressing for the Climate You Live In 115
  - The Dress 116
    - Wicking layer 116
    - Insulating layer 116
    - Protection layer 116
    - Headwear 116
    - Sunglasses and goggles 117
    - Gloves and mittens 117
    - Socks 117
- References 118
  - Other Resources of Emergency Preparedness Information 119

The prudent see danger and take refuge, but the simple keep going and suffer for it.
Proverbs 27:12

Before an emergency happens.....
PLAN.......PREPARE.......BE INFORMED

This manual will help you and your family PLAN for an emergency, PREPARE your home, supplies and equipment for an emergency, and BE INFORMED on what to do for the most likely emergencies to occur in our area. It will also provide essential information to neighbors or emergency personnel who may be trying to help your family.

We strongly encourage all families to regularly study and review in their Family Home Evenings the information contained in this manual. It is hoped that the manual will be kept in a place that will allow it to be consulted with ease in the time of emergency.

By adhering to these practices, we may be more properly assured of the Lord's promise "...*if ye are prepared, ye shall not fear.*" *(Doctrine and Covenants 38:30)*

It wasn't raining when Noah built the Ark

This manual has been prepared for, and is intended to be read primarily by, the active members of The Church of Jesus Christ of Latter-day Saints, but would be useful to anyone seeking to be more prepared and self-reliant.

Please Note:

The contents of this booklet are intended to assist individuals and families in coping with emergency preparations. However, final decisions on preparation for actions taken during an emergency are the sole responsibility of individuals. No one knows your needs or can take care of you better than you can-nor does anyone else have that responsibility. Information and examples contained within this booklet are provided for illustration and advice only. Therefore, no liability is assumed by the Editor or any of the Authors for the use or misuse of any information or products contained in this publication.

This publication has not been endorsed or produced by The Church of Jesus Christ of Latter-day Saints and its contents and the opinions it expresses are those of the Editor and the separate authors. While it should not be construed as an official church publication, significant effort has been made to ensure that all materials are in accordance with general church guidelines on food storage and family preparedness.

This book is a compilation of many different authors' works that have been gathered from the public domain of the Internet over the course of many years. These articles have been bound together and are presented here to simplify your access to them.

Special Acknowledgements

We wish to acknowledge as major sources for the information herein contained:
The wise Counsel of LDS Church Leaders over the years,
The Bozeman Montana Stake Presidency
LDS Preparedness Manual, prepared by Christopher M. Parrett
&
Individual Contributions of interested Church Members from throughout the world who contributed information via e-mail.

For general church guidelines on food storage and family preparedness, beliefs, and official policy of The Church of Jesus Christ of Latter-day Saints, please visit the following:

www.providentliving.org
www.lds.org

EMERGENCY BASICS

BEFORE AN EMERGENCY

1. Know how to turn off gas, water and electricity to your home

2. Know Basic First Aid

3. Have a "72 Hour Emergency Kit" readily available

4. Keep your car 1/2 full of gas.

5. Have a plan for reuniting your family one place right outside your home and another outside the immediate neighborhood.

6. Have an "out of area" contact person. Every family member needs to know the number or have it with them.

7. Have operational smoke alarms, carbon monoxide alarms and fire extinguishers installed.

8. Children at school - make sure your list of adults authorized to pick up your children

is current and complete. Tell older children who self transport to follow the instructions of authorities.

9. Know your neighbors, their skills and their needs. Plan how you could help each other special needs, elderly, disabled, child care if children come from school and parents cannot get home. Working together as neighbors can save lives and property.

10. Have a "Home Hazard Hunt" –
- Repair defective wiring and leaky gas connections
- Secure water heater with straps to stud walls
- Fasten shelves securely
- Place large heavy objects on lower shelves
- Hang pictures and mirrors away from beds

- Brace overhead light fixtures, china cabinets, bookcases, top heavy objects
- Store weed killers pesticides and flammable products away from heat
- Clean and repair chimneys, flue pipes, vent connections and gas vents
- Place oily rags or waste in covered metal cans
- Clear surrounding brush or weeds 30' from home
- Take care of anything that could move, fall, break, or cause a fire

DURING AN EMERGENCY

1. STAY CALM, REASSURE OTHERS (especially young children), THINK through the consequences of any action.

2. DO NOT TIE UP TELEPHONE LINES needed for emergency operations.

3. LISTEN to portable radio for ALL weather service advisories.

4. REMAIN INDOORS, stand in hallway, strong interior doorway or take cover under a desk or table away from glass.

5. FOLLOW ADVICE OF LOCAL AUTHORITIES.

If you are told to evacuate, do so promptly. If told to go to a certain location, go straight there and check in.

NOAA image

AFTER AN EMERGENCY

1. Check for injuries - provide First Aid.

2. Check for safety using a light stick or flashlight. Check for gas, water, or sewage breaks, check for downed electric lines and shorts. "Turn off appropriate utilities only if you suspect the lines are damaged or if you are instructed to do so. If you turn the gas off, you will need a professional to turn it back on." FEMA

3. Check for home hazards, fire dangers or dangerous spills. Be aware that spilled bleaches, gasoline and other liquids may produce deadly fumes when chemicals mix. Get advice from emergency personnel on how to clean up spilled liquids especially if there are noxious fumes.

4. Listen to the radio for specific instructions from Public Safety agencies. Local Media will announce change in school openings and closings

5. Wear shoes at all times, if possible.

6. Stay off the telephone except to report emergencies.

7. Check on neighbors especially the elderly, disabled or those with small children

8. After the emergency is over, let relatives know how and where you are.

IN CASE OF:

EARTHQUAKE

BEFORE:

Follow Emergency Basics 1-9 plus:

1. Know the earthquake plan for your children's school. Discuss it with them.

2. Have earthquake drills
- Identify safe spots in each room
- Act out getting to the safe spot in less than 2 seconds and covering your head
- Identify danger zones to stay away from bookcases, windows, furnishings that could fall
- Drill: Once per month have a child yell "EARTHQUAKE" - Everyone should respond then discuss choices made

DURING:

1. STAY CALM, REASSURE OTHERS: expect loud noises, sounds will come from the motion of the ground, the structure of the building, and from falling objects.

2. IF INSIDE: Stay inside and find protection in a doorway, hallway, under a desk or table, away from tall book shelves, or glass. Avoid (brick) masonry walls, chimneys fireplaces. Cover your head and face with anything handy (coat, blanket, cardboard) to shield from falling debris and splintering glass.

3. IF OUTSIDE: Stay there, move away from buildings, trees, power poles/lines. The greatest danger from falling debris is just outside doorways and close to outer walls.

4. IF DRIVING: Stop as soon as possible. Never stop on or under bridges, overpasses, under power lines or where buildings can fall on you, stay in the vehicle. A car is an excellent shock absorber, it will shake but is fairly safe. When you drive on watch for hazards

created by the earthquake such as fallen objects, downed power lines, broken or undermined roads.

5. IF IN AN OFFICE BUILDING: Stay next to a pillar or support column, under a heavy table or desk, away from windows. File cabinets should not open toward you.

6. IF AT A PUBLIC EVENT: theater/ athletic stadium: drop to the floor between the seats, cover your head, hold on and ride it out. DO NOT RUSH FOR THE EXITS as hundreds of others will do. Leave calmly, avoid elevators, watch for panic in crowds.

AFTER:

Be prepared for additional aftershocks.

1. Check for injuries - provide emergency First Aid. Do not try to move seriously injured persons.

2. Be prepared to respond to psychological needs created by the trauma of the experience. Stay with small children - they fear separation during times of stress.

3. Check for safety. Turn off appropriate utilities.

- Check for gas, water, sewage breaks.

- Check for downed electric lines and shorts.

- Check for fire hazards, chemical spills, toxic fumes. If there is leaking gas, leave the house and report to authorities.

- Check building for cracks around chimney and foundation.

- Open cabinets and closets carefully and be ready for falling objects

4. Flashlights or lightsticks are safe: Do not turn on electrical switches, light matches, or create sparks until you are sure there are no gas leaks.

5. Wear shoes - clean up dangerous spills and broken glass and debris.

6. Listen to the radio for specific instructions from Public Safety agencies.

7. Stay off the telephone except to report emergencies - put phones back on the hooks.

8. Stay out of severely damaged buildings, aftershocks may finish them off.

9. Confine or leash frightened pets.

10. NEVER ASSUME DOWNED POWER LINES ARE DEAD - or you may be! People, metal and damp objects are good electrical conductors. To avoid shock and serious burns stay back. If you are in your car, and live wires have fallen across the car, remain in your car until help arrives. If trying to rescue someone in contact with live wires, use a wooden pole or other non conductive material to move the wire.

11. Do not go sightseeing.

12. Notify family to let them know how and where you are. If you must leave, leave a message of your intended route and destination and who is with you.

POWER OUTAGE

BEFORE:

Know the location of electrical fuse box and circuit breaker.
- Have antifreeze.
- Have emergency supplies (water, food, first aid, flashlight, etc.)

DURING:

1. Unplug all major appliances. When the power comes on, the power surge could ruin appliances.
2. Report any downed power lines.
3. DO NOT OPEN the refrigerator and freezer
4. In case of long term power failure in the winter, you may need to winterize your home to protect your pipes from freezing.
- Shut off the water at the street.
- Drain all the water from your pipes at the lowest
faucet. Flush all toilets so there is nowater left in them.
- Turn off the gas to the water heater and drain it.
- Pour antifreeze in all drains, toilet bowls and toilet

tanks.

5. Leave for a location with power or stay in your home. If you stay, it is easier to heat one room than the whole house. Remember that heating/cooking equipment requiring gasoline, propane, white gas, coalman fuel or charcoal briquets should not be used inside.

AFTER:

1. When the power comes on, plug in appliances one by one to prevent overloading the system.

2. Turn the water back on. Be sure all taps are turned off first.

3. Check the food in the refrigerator/freezer. If the door is not opened, food in the refrigerator should stay cold up to 6 hours. Foods "warmer than refrigeration" temperatures more than 2 hours should be discarded. If food from the freezer is still as cold as refrigeration temperatures, it can be eaten but do not re-freeze. Meat that still has ice crystals can safely be re-frozen. If meat is thawed and "refrigeration cold", it can be cooked and eaten or refrozen. In a well filled freezer, food will have ice crystals for about 3 days.

HIGH WINDS

BEFORE:

1. Secure objects such as outdoor furniture, tools, trash cans, etc.
2. Have emergency supplies: water, food, first aid, etc.
3. Listen to the radio for weather updates.
4. Be prepared to board or tape up windows.
5. Open a window at the opposite end of the house about 1" to relieve pressure.

DURING:

Take shelter in center hallways, closets or basement areas away from windows. Avoid areas where flying objects may hit you.

AFTER:

Clean up. Windows: use duct tape and plastic to mend if cracked; plywood to board up if broken.

SEVERE THUNDER & LIGHTNING

INDOORS:

Stay away from open doors, windows, fireplaces. Close the curtains to protect you from shattered glass. Don't use electrical equipment (hair dryers, electric blankets, etc) during the storm. Don't use the telephone except for emergency. Lightning may strike telephone lines.

OUTDOORS:

Don't use metal objects (lawn mowers, fishing rods, golf clubs. Remove metal cleated golf shoes). Get out of the water and off of small boats. Avoid being the highest object in any area. If you feel an electrical charge (your hair stands on end or skin tingles) drop to the ground in a crouched position with hands on knees and your head between them. DO NOT lie flat on the ground.

FIRST AID:

1. Persons struck by lightning receive a severe electrical shock and may be burned where the lightning entered and left the body, but they can be handled safely, they carry no electrical charge.

2. A person struck by lightning can often be revived by prompt mouth to mouth resuscitation, cardiac massage and prolonged artificial respiration.

BLIZZARDS

Listen to weather advisories and avoid traveling in blizzard conditions if possible. If you are trapped in a car by a blizzard:

1. Stay in the vehicle, do not attempt to walk out; disorientation occurs quickly in blowing, drifting snow.

2. Avoid overexertion from trying to push the car out or shoveling heavy drifts.

3. Run the motor only about 10 minutes each hour for heat and only with a rear window slightly open for ventilation. Be cautious of carbon monoxide poisoning make sure the exhaust pipe does not become blocked with snow.

4. Make yourself visible: raise the hood, tie red cloth to the antenna.

5. Exercise by clapping hands, moving fingers, arms, legs to keep blood circulating. Change positions frequently.

6. Do not eat snow - it will lower your body temperature.

7. Keep watch - do not allow all occupants of the car to sleep at once.

FLOODS

BEFORE:

1. Find out if your residence is in a probable flood plain. Plan what to do, where to go.

2. Store emergency supplies: water, food, first aid, medications, documents, radio, flashlights etc.

3. Listen to the radio or TV for changing weather conditions.

4. Place sandbags, lumber, plastic sheeting etc. in strategic places. (Sandbags should be stacked away from building far enough to avoid damaging the walls.)

5. Make sure vehicle gas tanks are at least ½ full in case of evacuation.

6. Prepare for evacuation.

7. Move valuables to an upper floor or as high as possible.

DURING:

1. Stay calm.

2. If there is time, disconnect all gas and electric appliances. Shut off the main water valve to keep contaminated water from entering the house. Also shut off the power at the main breaker. Remember,

if you shut off the gas, a professional will have to come turn it back on.

3. If asked to evacuate, use travel routes recommended by local authorities to reach the Evacuation Center. Drive slowly in water, use low gear. If your car stalls, abandon it as soon as possible.

4. Listen for further instructions on the emergency frequency of your radio.

AFTER:

1. Do not return home until local authorities say that it is safe.

2. Check your home carefully for structural damage, gas leaks and downed electrical wires.

3. Don't use electrical appliances that have been flooded until repaired.

4. Don't use food that has been contaminated by flood waters.

5. Don't drink tap water until authorities say it is safe to do so.

6. Clean everything. Flood water carries contaminants and disease. Throw out all wet food, medicines and cosmetics.

FIRES

PREVENTION

1. Practice fire resistant housekeeping; discard rubbish, trash, oily rags in metal cans outside home. Use proper size fuses, replace frayed cords, don't overload electrical outlets.
2. Store flammable liquids outside the home in tightly closed metal containers.
3. Maintain smoke detectors and fire extinguishers in working order.
4. Keep garden hose near the faucet, especially in the winter when fire danger is the greatest
5. Keep oak brush, weeds, etc., cut back at least 30' from the house

BASIC FIREFIGHTING

1. Keep an escape route between you and the fire.
2. Point the fire retardant at the base of the fire, where the flames meet the fuel in a sweeping motion.

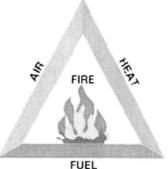

3. If your clothes catch on fire: STOP! DROP!, & ROLL!!
4. Escape: Have two ways out of every room. GET OUT FAST! Don't stop to dress, gather pets, valuables or toys. Smoke and toxic gasses rise and can kill you in minutes. Crawl on your hands and knees. Take short small breaths. Cover mouth with a cloth if possible. If a door is hot, do not open it. Keep doors and windows closed. ONCE OUT - STAY OUT!
5. Have a pre-arranged meeting place outside. When 2 people arrive, one should leave to call the fire department. The 2nd stays to tell the family the 1st has gone so no one tries to go back in to find him.

TYPES OF FIRES

Electrical fires: Be sure to shut off the electricity first. Then put out the flames with an extinguisher, water or other fire retardant. IF YOU CAN'T SHUT OFF THE ELECTRICITY, DO NOT USE WATER ON AN ELECTRICAL FIRE.

Oil, Grease, or Gasoline Fire: Smother the flames. Use your fire extinguisher, a lid, bread board, salt, baking soda, or earth. DO NOT USE WATER. In a gas fire, shut off the gas supply. Use a fire extinguisher, water, sand, or earth to smother the flame.

CHEMICAL SPILL

Hazardous Materials are chemical substances, which, if released or misused, can pose a threat to our health and/or environment. This scenario is most likely in the case of a tanker spill on the highway.

ON THE SCENE:

1. If you witness a Chemical emergency, stay clear of the chemical and vapors or smoke. CALL 911.

2. If you are in a vehicle, close the windows, turn off the air systems, and leave the area.

NOTIFICATION:

Orders to Evacuate or Shelter-In-Place may be given if there is a threat to the community. You may be notified by:

1. City Watch - a reverse 911 system with a prerecorded message.

2. A knock on the door by uniformed fire or police personnel or by CERT volunteers.

3. An announcement by loud speaker from an official police or fire department vehicle.

4. The Emergency Alert System on TV or Radio.

5. Sirens at a local refinery or business.

6. Neighborhood block captain. IF YOUR NEIGHBORS TELL YOU THEY RECEIVED NOTIFICATION, IT PROBABLY APPLIES TO YOU, TOO!

EVACUATE

If you are requested to evacuate, directions may be provided for safe routes to follow. Go to a designated shelter - "reception center" to check in then you may go to another safe location (home of a relative or friend, motel etc).

2. Take 72 hour kits - include all necessary medications for extended period of time.

3. Shut off all appliances.

4. Leash or cage pets and/or take them with you, if possible. However, most shelters will not accept pets.

5. Lock all doors and windows. Leave a message as to where you have gone.

6. Follow given evacuation routes.

SHELTER-IN-PLACE

This is a method of protecting yourself, family and small pets from the effects of a released chemical.

1. If possible, bring pets inside.

2. Go inside, close and lock all doors and windows to the outside.

3. Turn off all heating/air conditioning systems and switch vents to the "closed" position.

4. Close all fire place dampers.

5. Go to one room and

- Use a basement room only as a last resort. Some chemicals are heavier than air and may seep into basements.

- Choose a room with a bathroom attached if possible.

- Seal all windows, doors, and vents with plastic sheeting, wax paper, or other material and tape. Include spaces around pipes.

- Place damp towels under doorways

- Close the drapes/shades over windows and stay away from the windows.

6. Remain in place until you are told by police or fire personnel or through radio/TV broadcasts that it is safe to leave.

7. When the chemical emergency is over, open all doors and windows for ventilation.

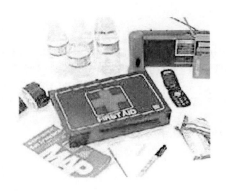

72 HOUR EMERGENCY KIT

The objective of the Family 72-Hour Emergency Preparedness Kit is to have, previously assembled and placed in one location, all of those essential items you and your family will need during a 72-hour time period following an emergency. When an emergency occurs you will probably not have the luxury of going around the house gathering up needed items, especially if you have to evacuate your home on short notice.

Take time now to gather whatever your family needs to survive for three days (72 Hours) based upon the assumption that those items are the only possessions you will have. Store these kits in a closet near the front door or some other easily accessible place where they can be quickly and easily grabbed on the way out the door.

Pack all items in plastic Zip-loc type bags to keep them dry and air tight. Keep a list of the dates when certain items need to be reviewed, especially foods, outgrown clothing and medications so that they may be properly rotated.

You or family members may also have "Special Needs" that have to be addressed.- i.e. Indigent, Baby, Medical needs, etc.

Remember, this is a TEMPORARY, short term kit. Other "Kits" you should have will be for your vehicle, business location, school, or places you and family members may spend a majority of the day away from home. You should also be preparing for your "Long-Term" needs with your Home Storage.

Container

The container you choose for your kit must be waterproof, have some type of carrying handle, and must be able to be carried easily by family members. The portability of your kit is very important. Wherever possible reduce any extra bulk and weight from your kit. It's likely you will have to carry the your 72 hour kit for a considerable distance / time.

Water

Advised amounts of water for a kit vary. It is recommended to have a minimum of two quarts per day for each adult. However, a person can survive quite well on less, and the load of carrying six quarts of water with a pack is great. Outdoor survival course veterans agree that a two-liter bottle should be adequate. Water purification tablets or crystals need to be a part of each kit. Refer to Emergency Water Supply for treatment methods and information on portable water filters. Before you leave your house or evacuate be sure to drink plenty of water. This will help you stay hydrated and also help your water supply last longer.

Food

You should include in your kit a three-day supply of non-perishable food. The food items should be compact and lightweight, in sealed packages. MRE's (Meals Ready to Eat) are a good choice because they require little or no preparation. Freeze-dried foods are lightweight but require extra water in your kit. Canned goods are heavy with extra refuse. Plan nutritionally balanced meals, keeping in mind that this is a survival kit. Include vitamins or other supplements, if desired. *Possible foods for a kit might include:*

- MRE's - snack crackers - hard candy
- dried fruits- instant oatmeal – powdered milk
- jerky - bouillon cubes - raisins/nuts
- instant rice - dried soups - gum
- granola bars- instant pudding - powdered drinks

Also include a mess kit or other compact equipment for cooking and eating. A can opener may also be useful.

Shelter

The objective of shelter is to provide emergency housing. It is extremely important to be physically protected from nature's weather elements. There are many types of shelter that can be easily included in your 72-hour kit. You may want to consider family tent, backpacker's tent, tube tent, rain poncho, garbage bags, nylon rope or cord, duct tape, space blanket and space sleeping bag.

Bedding

- Bedding should be warm, lightweight, comfortable, waterproof and compact.
- Blankets can be used to make a bed roll but generally they are not as comfortable nor as warm as a sleeping bag. Wool blankets are the best since they retain their warming ability even when wet. However, blankets are very heavy and bulky.
- Space blankets and space bags (aluminum coated mylar) are very efficient at retaining body heat and are a must for every 72-hour kit. Even when used by themselves, without the added benefit of a sleeping bag they will keep you warm during the night. In cold winter weather they may not be entirely comfortable but they will probably keep you warm enough to keep you alive. Being plastic, however, they are impervious to moisture. This is good for keeping out rain but they also retain sweat and condensation from your breath. You may find that periodically during the night you will have to air them out in order to sleep comfortably. They can also be used during the day to protect from rain, sun and to retain body warmth.

Clothing

Include in your kit one change of clothing and footwear, preferably work clothing. Anticipate severe weather conditions. If you have a growing family remember to update clothing sizes and needs at least once a year.

Try to avoid wearing cotton clothing. Tight cotton clothing holds water next to the skin. Wet inner clothing causes freezing. Cotton clothing "wicks" (draws water up the very small individual fibers), thus retaining water and spreading it over the entire body, causing loss of body heat at an ever greater rate. Wool clothing is best. Wool is a natural thermostatic insulator that keeps you warm in the winter and cool in the summer. Wool is naturally durable and can withstand rugged and tough wear. Wool also repels water and has the unique property of keeping the body warm even if it does get wet. Wool dries from the inside out and does not "wick." Include two pairs of wool socks- one pair for wearing and one for keeping your feet warm while sleeping.

Fuel

Every family member should have fire starting materials and know how to start a fire. Several of these items should be assembled into a kit and labeled as "fire starting kit." Teach all family members how to use them and let them practice building fires with all methods until they feel totally confident with their ability to do so. Even little children aged five or six can be safely instructed in correct fire building techniques under proper supervision. Then if an emergency arises, they will not panic or feel overwhelmed or frightened at the prospect of building a fire for their warmth and protection.

Some different sources are:

- **Matches.** Carry at least two dozen wooden kitchen matches that have been either dipped in wax or nail polish to make them waterproof or carry them in a waterproof container.

- **Metal match**. Waterproof, fireproof, durable, and non-toxic. Will light thousands of fires. Available at sporting goods stores.

- **Butane lighters**, such as Bic cigarette lighters, are excellent ways to light a fire.

-**Magnesium** fire starters are good for starting fires with wet or damp wood. Shave magnesium shavings off of a magnesium block with a pocket knife and then strike a spark from a flint starter with a pocket knife. Magnesium burns exceptionally hot and will ignite almost any combustible material. Works even when wet and can be purchased at most sporting goods stores.

- **Small magnifying glass**. Use to concentrate sunlight onto paper, shredded bark or other tinder.

- **Steel wool**. Fine steel wool (used for scrubbing pots and pans- but not Brillo pads or other types that have soap in them) can be used for tinder. Hold two "D" flashlight cells together in one hand (or one 9-volt transistor radio battery) while touching one end of a clump of steel wool to the positive end of the battery and the other end of the steel wool to the negative end of the battery. The current causes the steel wool fibers to incandesce and then produce a flame. It burns very hot and fairly fast so have lots of other tinder to burn once the steel wool ignites.

-**Candles** can be used for warmth, light, and starting fires. To start a fire simply cut a piece of candle about 1/2 inch in length and place it on top of the tinder. When lit the wax will run over the tinder making it act as a wick and ignite. You can also place small twigs and other easily burnable materials directly into the fame to build a fire.

- **Car Battery**. If you are near your car you can easily put sparks into tinder by attaching any wires to the battery posts and scraping the ends together in the tinder.

First Aid Kit

Update your first aid skills. Keep your first aid kit well-supplied.

Suggested first-aid supplies for 72-hour kit:

First-Aid book	Waterproof container
Assortment of band-aids	Gauze pads
Butterfly bandages	Cotton balls
Small roll of gauze	Adhesive tape
Cotton swabs	Safety pins
Pepto-bismol tablets	Antacid tablets
Cold pack	Consecrated oil
Hydrogen peroxide	Alcohol (disinfectants)
Smelling salts	Medicine dropper
Tweezers	Alcohol wipes
Benadryl capsules	
Asprin (promotes healing of burns)	
Tylenol (chewable for children)	
Collapsible scissors	Thermometer
Crushable heat pack	Prescriptions
Small tube of antiseptic cream	
Small spool of thread	Two needles

Miscellaneous

Some other miscellaneous items that may be very helpful are:

Light stick	Small flashlight
Extra batteries	Pocket handwarmer
Compact fishing kit	Compass / map
Pocket knife	50 ft nylon cord
Plastic poncho	Garbage bag(s)
Paper or cards	Pen, pencil
Fine wire	Extra plastic bags
Small scriptures	Favorite songs
Small game, toy, etc.	Spare glasses
Money (small bills)	Field glasses
Toothbrush/paste	Metal mirror
Comb	Razor
Pre-moistened wipes	Toilet paper
Feminine products	Sunscreen
Soap	Lip balm with sunscreen
Bandana	
Soap (waterless, bar)	
Identification/medical cards	
Special items for kids comfort	
Portable radio with batteries	

Family Information Record

In addition to emergency survival supplies you should also collect vital family information. Record and keep it in at least two safe places-a fire resistant "get-away" box that you can take with you if you have to leave the home, and a safe-deposit box at your bank or credit union.

The following items would be useful for you to record and keep in these two locations:

- Genealogy records

- Full name and social security numbers of all family members

- Listing of vehicles, boats etc. with identification and license numbers

- Listing of all charge account card numbers and expiration dates, bank account numbers (both checking and saving), insurance policy numbers, securities, deeds, and loan numbers showing the company name, address and telephone numbers.

- Name, address, and telephone number for each of the following:

employer, schools, fire/paramedics, family contacts,

utility company, police, doctor, hospital,

attorney, civil defense

- Location of important documents

insurance policies, deeds, securities, licenses, loans, will, safe-deposit box key, vehicle titles (pink slips), birth/death certificates, social security I.D. cards, citizenship papers, letter of instruction, tax returns (last 5 years)

Infants

When assembling items for your 72-hour kit, be sure to include all necessary items for infants. It would be a good idea to include a separate back pack or other container that holds nothing but infant supplies (which can be surprisingly voluminous). This kit should be kept with the kits of other family members so that it will not be forgotten in a moment of haste. As the baby begins to grow, replace clothing and diapers with the next larger size

Car Mini-Survival Kit

Your car is frequently your home away from home. Most of us spend many hours in our cars each month. Anything from a jammed-up freeway to a major disaster could force you to rely on your car for short-term shelter and survival. It is a wise practice to keep simple provision for emergencies in your car. A self-made cold-weather car kit, as described in some preparedness stores, is also good to keep in the car.

At-Work Survival Kit

Many persons stand a 40 percent chance of being at work when an earthquake or other emergency strikes. A mini-survival kit kept at your place of work could make the hours until you are able to get home more comfortable and safer. This kit could be a duplicate of the car mini-survival kit.

Notes

Update your 72 Hour Kit every six months (put a note in your calendar/planner) to make sure that: all food, water, and medication is fresh and has not expired; clothing fits; personal documents and credit cards are up to date; and batteries are charged. Small toys/games are important too as they will provide some comfort and entertainment during a stressful time.

You can include any other items in your 72 Hour Kit that you feel are necessary for your family's survival.

FIRST AID BASICS

Our Church leaders admonish "All members of the Church should be trained in basic first-aid skills" (*Preparing and Responding to Emergencies: Guidelines for Church Leaders*).

You are likely to encounter an emergency needing first aid attention several times during your life. Families with young children are constantly being subjected to situations in which injury may occur and your quick calm thinking and application of first aid principles may make the difference between life and death.

Automobile accidents account for slightly more than one-half of all accidental deaths occurring each year. Your knowledge of first aid could not only save a member of your immediate family, but could also save the life of a total stranger. This chapter is not intended to teach you all you need to know about first aid. Such knowledge can only be obtained by attending first aid training courses sponsored by the American Red Cross or other training organizations and/or by extensively reading and studying books on first aid.

Emergency Care

Depending on the type of emergency, you will have to make a quick decision of what to do first and what not to do.

1. Keep the victim lying down his head level with body until you have made some assessment of the problem.

- If the victim is in severe shock place on back with legs slightly elevated.

- If victim is vomiting or bleeding from the mouth and is semi-conscious there is danger of victim aspirating this material, place him on his side.

- Shortness of breath-- if victim has a chest injury, place him in a sitting or semi-sitting position, or position of comfort.

2. Examine the victim for hemorrhage (serious bleeding), asphyxiation (suspended breathing), and shock-- all of which require immediate treatment.

The primary survey covers these four areas:

- Open airway.

- Check breathing.

- Check circulation.

- Stop hemorrhage or severe bleeding.

3. Do not move the victim more than is absolutely necessary. Remove clothing only enough to determine the extent of injuries. It is preferable to rip or cut clothing to remove it (removing in conventional manner may compound the injuries if they are severe).

4. Keep the victim reassured and as comfortable as possible.

5. If the victim's injury is extensive, it is best not to let them see it.

6. Do not touch open wounds.

7. Do not give unconscious persons any solids or liquids by mouth.

8. Do not move the victim unless necessary to prevent further harm or injury. If you must move the victim, do it keeping the lengthwise axis of the body straight. Keep the victim warm, but not overly hot. Remember, by far the greater number of injuries will require a minimum of effort on your part and a maximum of judgment and self control to prevent doing too much.

In emergency situations, rapid, calm, efficient efforts can minimize problems; and even in prolonged emergency situations, sticking with standard first aid care may be better than risking life threatening procedures.

Immediate Lifesaving Measures

Most injuries can be dealt with calmly and without hurry. However, in serious life threatening injuries first steps must be taken immediately to preserve life.

-First, open the victim's airway and restore his breathing and heartbeat if necessary

-Second, Stop any bleeding and dress and bandage wounds to prevent infection.

-Third, treat the victim for poisoning, and

-Fourth, treat him for shock.

Communicable Disease / Pandemic

Communicable Diseases are illnesses caused by microorganisms and transmitted from an infected person or animal to another person or animal. Most diseases are spread through contact or close proximity because the bacteria or viruses are airborne; i.e., they can be expelled from the nose and mouth of the infected person and inhaled by anyone in the vicinity. Such diseases include diphtheria, scarlet fever, measles, mumps, whooping cough, influenza, and smallpox.

This information refers to influenza and a possible influenza pandemic. Influenza, more commonly refered to as the Flu, refers to illnesses caused by a number of different influenza viruses. The flu can cause a range of symptoms and effects, from mild to lethal.

Two strains of flu, seasonal flu, and the H1N1 (Swine) flu, are currently circulating in the United States. A third, highly lethal H5N1 (Bird) flu is being closely tracked overseas.

How to protect your Family

-Know what the flu looks like- Fever >100F, sore throat, coughing and sneezing, body aches, and headache.

-Wear a mask and/or cover your cough and sneezes.

-Dispose of tissues in the trash.

-Wash your hands after coughing, sneezing or touching your face. Alcohol gels work well for this.

-Evaluate whether you need to seek medical attention (limit exposing others).

-Keep a distance from well patients in waiting areas.

-Stay home when you are ill.

How the flu is spread

-Droplets are produced by coughing, sneezing, talking, and laughing.

-Droplets can travel 3-6 feet

-Touching your eyes, nose and mouth with contaminated hands

-Virus can live on surfaces for up to 2 hours

-Most adults can spread the virus 1 day prior to symptom onset

-It takes 1-4 days for symptoms to develop after exposure.

Personal Hygiene Basics

The best way to stop the spread of germs that cause the flu or other illnesses that can be spread from one person to another is to wash hands often and control the discharges associated with coughing and sneezing. According to the U.S. Centers for Disease Control Prevention, "Hand washing is the single most important means of preventing the spread of infection." Hands should be washed with clean water and soap:

- When they are dirty
- After using the restroom
- Before and after preparing meals
- After cutting and handling uncooked meat
- Before eating
- After cleaning the house
- After caring for someone who is ill
- After changing an infant's diaper
- After cleaning up blood or body fluids
- After handling soiled bed linens and clothes
- Before and after flossing teeth
- After you cough or sneeze in them

How to Wash Hands

1. Adjust water to a comfortable level and wet hands. Dispense a small amount of soap into the palms of the hands creating lather.

2. Using as much friction as needed, thoroughly clean all surfaces of hands including between the fingers.

3. Pay attention to the nails and nail beds by rubbing the nails of one hand across the palm of the other, creating enough friction to clean underneath the nails. Hands should be washed for at least 20 seconds. Use of a memory aid, such as singing a song or reciting a

familiar poem, may assist individuals in washing for an adequate period of time.

4. Rinse the hands under running water, being sure to hold the hands in a downward position.

5. Use paper towels to thoroughly dry the hands.

6. Using the same paper towel, turn off the water supply and open the door.

Other Hand Cleaning Options

Alcohol-based hand cleaners can also be used to clean hands. Put a small amount on the hands and rub all hand surfaces until the hands are dry. If commercially prepared alcohol-based hand cleaners are not available or are too costly, an alcohol- based hand cleaner can be made by mixing 70% alcohol and glycerin (about 2% by volume of glycerin). The glycerin keeps the hands soft because the alcohol can dry them out. Hands will periodically need to be washed with soap and water because the hands will have a glycerin buildup with time.

Cough and Sneeze Etiquette

The following measures to contain respiratory secretions are recommended for all individuals with signs and symptoms of a respiratory infection.

- Cover the nose and mouth when coughing or sneezing.

- Provide and encourage use of tissues to contain respiratory secretions. If possible, dispose of tissues immediately in the nearest no-touch waste receptacle after use.

- If tissues are unavailable, cough or sneeze into a handkerchief or your arm or shoulder, not your hands.

- If you cough or sneeze in your hands, be sure to wash or clean them with an alcohol-based hand cleaner as soon as possible to stop the spread of germs.

Preparing for a Pandemic Influenza Outbreak

The Self Imposed Reverse Isolation (SIRQ) Plan

Protecting the Family – Building a Safe Haven

Protecting the family from the influenza virus is central to the plan. This requires that families sequester themselves from the outside world in order to avoid infection.

- Children should not go to school or play with friends.

- Parents should work from home as much as possible.

- The family should not attend public events (sporting events, cultural events, religious services, etc.).

-If family members do have to leave sequestration, they must be educated and committed to maintaining protection.

Instructions for Parents

-Must establish their home as a protected cell.

-Must understand that as long as their family is sequestered they are safe, but safety is only good AS LONG AS EVERY FAMILY MEMBER REMAINS SAFE AND DOES NOT BRING THE INFECTION HOME.

-Must understand the importance of not allowing children to interact with others outside the family during the time the plan is in place.

-Must know how to remain safe when they leave the home like using the proper protective equipment, and using protective methods of interacting in an infectious environment.

- Must have their homes prepared for a disruption in services.

Instructions for Children

- Are at high risk for transmission of disease because of less than ideal hygiene, close contact with others in closed environments, inadequate hand washing, etc.

- Need to be sequestered in family groups.

- Need to be isolated from others who are potentially infected.

- Need to be trained in methods of protecting themselves from infection at their level.

Protecting the Individual

- During an influenza pandemic, any individual that has to interact with the outside world must consider all they come in contact with as being infected.

- Individuals must know how to interact in such an environment.

- Individuals need education and training about how to protect themselves.

- Individuals need protective equipment to allow them to interact.

Protecting the Community

- Community leadership must support the SIRQ plan and strongly encourage its implementation

- Educate leaders, families and individuals about the plan.

- Implementation of reverse quarantine protection early (BEFORE THE INFECTION HITS THE COMMUNITY).

- Cancellation of schools, meetings, public venues, etc. (BEFORE THE INFECTION STARTS)

- Identify key services and individuals essential to these services.

- Provide or strongly encourage personal protection use in all essential sectors early.

- Plan on contingencies

- Provide venues for education of individuals and families.

- Facilitate obtaining protective equipment for individuals or groups.

- Lead by example.

This plan can be implemented without government or community support. A family or individual could use this plan and protect themselves as long as they are willing to keep themselves separate.

Public Utilities in an Emergency

Gas

-Locate your gas meter shutoff valve and learn how to turn the gas off.

-If you suspect the shut off valve may be corroded and not working properly, call your utility company for an operational check of the valve.

-Ensure a wrench is immediately available for turning the gas meter off in an emergency.

-If you smell natural gas, get everyone out and away from the home immediately. Do not use matches, lighter, open flame appliances or operate electrical switches. Sparks could ignite gas causing an explosion.

-Seek the assistance of a plumber to repair gas pipe damage.

Gas Shut-off

Water

-Label the water shut off valve and learn to turn off the water supply to your home. Identify the valve with a large tag. Ensure valve can be fully turned off. If the water valve requires the use of a special tool, make sure the tool is readily available.

-Shut off the main valve to prevent contamination of the water supply in your water heater and plumbing.

Water Shut-off

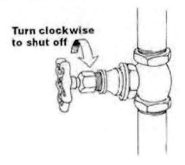

Sewer

-Your sewer system could be damaged in a disaster such as an earthquake, landslide or flood. Make sure the system is functioning as designed before using it to prevent contamination of your home and possibly the drinking water supply.

-Have a bucket or portable toilet available for disposing of human waste. Plastic bags placed in the toilet bowl will also work.

Electricity

-Locate your main electrical switch or fuse panel and learn how to turn the electrical power off.

-Remember, electrical sparks can cause a fire or explosion.

-If you are using a generator as a backup power supply, remember to:

-Follow the generator manufacturer's instructions.

-Connect lights and appliances directly to the generator and not the electrical system. (Generators connected to a utility company's electrical system must be inspected by the utility and the state electrical inspector. Failure to have the system inspected may result in death or injury to utility crews trying to restore service to the area)

Breaker Panel

Switch breakers to "OFF"
to shut off individual circuits

Blanks for additional circuits

Fire Safety

Getting Prepared

- Install smoke detectors according to the manufacturer's directions, on every level of your house: outside bedrooms on the ceiling or high on the wall, at the top of open stairways, or at the bottom of enclosed stairs and near (but not in) the kitchen.

- Clean smoke detectors once a month and change batteries at two specified times each year (when you set your clocks for Daylight Savings or Standard Time for example).

- Plan two escape routes out of each room. Contact your local fire authority for help in planning for the safe escape of those with disabilities.

- Make sure windows are not nailed or painted shut and security grating on windows have a fire safety opening feature.

- Teach everyone to stay low to the floor when escaping from a fire.

- Pick a meeting place outside your home for the family to meet after escaping from a fire. ONCE OUT, STAY OUT!

- Practice your escape plans at least twice a year.

- Clean out storage areas. Store flammable and combustible liquids in approved containers. Keep containers in the garage or an outside storage area.

- Inspect electrical appliances and extension cords for bare wires, worn plugs and loose connections annually.

- Clean and inspect primary and secondary heating equipment annually.

- Learn how to turn off the gas and electricity in an emergency.

- Install A-B-C type fire extinguishers: teach family members how to use them.
- Inspect or service your fire extinguisher annually.

In case of Fire

- Do not attempt to extinguish a fire that is rapidly spreading.
- Use water or a fire extinguisher to put out small fires.
- Never use water on a electrical fire.
- Smother oil and grease fires in the kitchen with baking soda or salt, or put a lid over the flame if it is burning in a pan.
If your clothes catch fire — Stop–Drop–Roll — until the fire is out.
- Sleep with your door closed.
- If the smoke alarm sounds, crouch down low, feel the bottom of the door with the palm of your hand before opening it. If the door is hot, escape through the window. If the door is not hot and this route is your only means of escape, crawl below the level of the smoke and use the first available exit door to escape. If you cannot escape, leave the door closed, stay where you are and hang a white or light-colored sheet outside the window.

After a Fire

- Stay out of the burned structure.
- Notify your local disaster relief service if you need housing, food, etc.
- Call your insurance agent.
- Ask the fire department for assistance in retrieving important documents.
- Keep records of all clean-up and repair costs.
- Secure personal belongings.
- If you are a tenant, notify the landlord.

Self Reliance

Nothing can bring you peace but yourself.
Nothing can bring you peace but the triumph of principles.
~ Ralph Waldo Emerson

The Lord has commanded that we use the blessings we have been given to become self reliant as individuals and families. The gospel of Jesus Christ requires that we take individual responsibility for our own spiritual and temporal well-being. We are expected to learn and practice principles of self reliance.

As we gain better understanding of these principles, we will seek ways to apply them in our daily lives and commit to improve to become more self-reliant. The gospel plan requires individual effort and responsibility.

Three areas are essential to our temporal wellbeing: home production and storage, personal and family finances, and physical health.

Home Storage

We have been advised to acquire and store a reserve of basic food and water that will sustain our lives during difficult times or in emergencies. By following this counsel, we will help protect ourselves if adversity comes. Through careful planning and faithful efforts, we can gradually store a supply of food according to our circumstances. Begin modestly by purchasing a few extra items of food that are part of your normal family diet. You can do it when you do your normal grocery shopping. Take advantage of items that are on sale.

Here are just a few other ideas:

- Complete a three-day supply of basic food items and then build your storage to a one-week supply.

- Gradually increase it until you have a one-month supply, two month supply, three-month supply.

- Consider items that will keep and store well, such as wheat, beans, rice and canned goods.

- Concentrate on essentials.

- Create a rotating system to avoid spoilage.

- Water should be stored in leak-proof containers and should be kept away from heat sources.

- Prepare a 72-hour emergency kit for each family member and keep them within easy reach.

- Be prudent. Don't go to extreme measures to store food. Be obedient and faithful, and God will sustain you through trials.

We are familiar with the story of Joseph in Egypt and how he advised Pharaoh to prepare by storing grain during the seven years of plenty for the seven years of famine that would follow. This storage plan not only helped the people of Egypt, but it also blessed Joseph's own family. We don't know if such conditions might come again, but our leaders have advised us to prepare to meet an emergency and to survive economic downturns.

Personal and Family Finances

An economic crisis is often the result of poor financial planning and management. The two overriding principles of sound financial management are: first, live within your means, and second save for a rainy day.

What does it mean to live within your means, and how do you do it? It simply means to ensure that your expenses are less than your income.

1. Begin by paying an honest tithing and a generous offering.

2. Avoid unnecessary debt. Discipline yourself to stay within your ability to pay when you must incur necessary debt. Then get out of debt as soon as you can and honor your commitments by paying on time. Interest increases your debt.

3. Establish a budget and use it. Involve family members (husband, wife, and children) in creating a budget and setting family financial goals. Learn to differentiate between needs and wants. Prioritize essential needs and take care of them first. Keep a record of expenditures and follow your plan.

Adjust if needed, but don't allow nonessential requests to disrupt your budget plans.

4. Take good care of personal belongings and teach family members frugality and thrift. Teach your children the old adage, "Use it up, wear it out, make it do or do without." Teach older children and teens to work, pay tithing and save.

5. Divide up your expenditures according to necessity. For example, ten percent of your income goes to tithing, thirty percent towards housing, ten percent to savings, etc.

6. Budget for irregular expenses such as car registration, insurance, birthdays, etc. The second principle is to save for a rainy day. Keep in mind that small sums saved regularly, over time, compound into large sums of money. Financial advisors agree that saving at least 10 percent of your income will provide flexibility and security in your future. You may want to:

- Save money to purchase more expensive items instead of getting them on credit.

- Gradually build a financial reserve to be used for emergencies.

- Set aside an amount for future family requirements such as missions and college education.

- Establish a retirement plan. Take advantage of all available plans that facilitate retirement planning, such as 401K matching plans, IRAs, and others.

Physical Health

Habits that contribute to our physical health are:
- Eating nutritious meals.
- Exercising regularly.
- Getting adequate sleep.
- Practicing hygiene and sanitation.
- Avoiding substance abuse.

A balanced diet includes fruits and vegetables, dairy products, grains, and protein. A good diet helps us stay healthy. Health specialists say that being overweight increases the risk of many diseases. They recommend a balanced diet and regular exercise to help us maintain proper body weight. Picky eaters should explore enough foods in order to-at the very least-adequately provide nutrition to their bodies. Seek professional help if you observe habits of eating and purging, or not eating altogether in any family member. These are signs of eating disorders that must be addressed. Regular exercise such as walking is important in maintaining physical fitness, good health, and a sense of well-being. Adequate sleep allows for repair and restoration of body cells. A California human population study reported that people who had seven to eight hours of sleep a day were healthier than those who slept six hours or less and those who slept nine hours or more. Seven to eight hours is best.

Keeping our homes and surroundings clean and sanitary will contribute to good health. Teach family members the habit of washing hands often, especially before eating.

The misuse of any substance that leads to dependency or addiction can destroy our physical, mental and spiritual well-being. This includes misuse of prescription and over the counter medications.

To be self-reliant in these areas, we should:

- Assess current circumstances.
- Set realistic goals.
- Identify available resources.
- Make specific plans to reach goals, and follow such plans.

Being self-reliant increases our ability to serve others, to assist the needy, and to give support and understanding to the emotionally-starved. Through righteous living, gospel study, and loving family relationships, we can achieve self-reliance and family preparedness, which will help us solve many of life's problems.

Gardening for Self Reliance

Planting a garden, even a small one, allows for a greater degree of self-reliance. With the right information and a little practice, individuals and entire families can enjoy the many benefits of planting and tending a garden.

Planning a Garden

As you begin to plan and prepare for a garden, here are a few general reminders:

-Vegetables need at least six hours of sunlight a day. The garden site should be relatively level. If there is a steep slope, run rows of plants across it to prevent erosion.

- It is a good idea to spade (mix) the soil to a depth of 12 to 14 inches. Adding organic matter such as manure, peat moss or leaves will benefit the soil. Be careful with fertilizer. All fertilizers have a three-digit code. For vegetable gardens, look for 8- 8-8 or 16-16-16.

- The simplest way to eliminate plant pests is to remove insects, worms, or eggs by hand. Some shake-on powder or liquid bug sprays are relatively safe to use.

- Proper depth for planting seeds is approximately four times as deep as the seed is thick. If you don't have a traditional garden plot, you can plant vegetables and herbs in containers that fit on driveways, balconies, roofs, and even window sills. This activity can be interesting and rewarding for adults and children alike. The following resources provide useful information about gardening in containers.

WHERE SHOULD I PLANT MY GARDEN?

Your garden should be close to home or work and easily accessible. You'll soon grow tired of commuting to a distant location. If you have no usable soil, you can build open-bottom containers on top of almost anything—even driveways, patios, and roofs. Choose a location that receives full sunlight all day long (or at least from mid-morning through the afternoon). Avoid trees, buildings, tall fences, hedges, and bushes that would block out the sun. Shade retards plant growth. For better results and less work, choose a level area. A slight southern slope (toward the sun) is ideal. Avoid north slopes (away from the sun). They have more shadows, less direct sunlight, and are sometimes too cold. If your ground is on a hillside, plant on the contour. Always level the ground under the containers. Locate your garden near a readily available source of good water. Do not use low spots where drainage is poor. Plants must have oxygen and will suffocate in standing water. Avoid windy areas, or build windbreaks. Tender plant leaves are easily damaged by strong winds. Fence the area to protect against animal and human intruders. If small animals are a problem, use wire mesh at ground

level.

HOW BIG SHOULD MY GARDEN BE?

Available sunny space often dictates the size of your garden. A small, well-tended, sunlit garden will yield more than a larger garden in poor conditions. Container dimensions:

- For two rows of plants, containers are ideally 10' long, 18" wide, and 8" high.

- Placing two rows of plants close together reduces watering and fertilizing by 50%.

- Include a 3' to 3 ½' aisle between containers, and at least one end aisle of 5'.

- Wide aisles give ready access to plants for feeding, watering, inspection, and harvesting. Start small and provide regular care, and your success will give you the training and incentive to increase your garden size.

HOW SHOULD I ARRANGE MY PLANTING AREA?

First create a blueprint of your garden area on scaled grid paper, showing the number, location, and size of your containers. Orient your containers for maximum advantage of sunlight, watering, and access. As you place plants on your blueprint, put tallest varieties on the north and east sides. Never shade short plants with taller ones. If necessary, place leafy crops, such as lettuce and spinach, in locations with less optimal sunshine.

WHAT SHOULD I PLANT?

Choose varieties that do well in your climate. If you live in a cooler northern climate, do not try to grow long-season crops like peanuts or sweet potatoes. Plan for only those vegetables that your family will eat, and only in quantities you can use, preserve, give away, or sell quickly, while fresh. Single-crop varieties like lettuce, broccoli, and cauliflower mature all at once, and so must be used quickly. Don't grow too much of these! Ever-bearing crops like pole beans, cucumbers, eggplant, peppers, squash, and tomatoes mature a little at a time, feed you all season long, and have a high value for the amount of space used, especially if grown vertically. Single-crop varieties that are grown for storage may be important for your winter emergency preparedness. Consider fall potatoes, cabbage, onions, winter squash, and carrots. Cool storage (40–50 degrees Fahrenheit) will preserve these vegetables. You can grow two crops of many single-crop varieties if you learn to grow and transplant healthy seedlings.

WHEN SHOULD I PLANT?

Proper planting time depends on your garden's climate and growing season.

-Your growing season is related to the time between the last spring frost and the first fall frost.

-Planting time is determined by (1) the average date of last frost and (2) the hardiness—or frost tolerance— of the crop you're planting.

-Find out the average day of last frost for your garden area from your County Extension Office or a computer database. Vegetable plants are classified into 4 levels of hardiness:

- Hardy plants can handle frost and cold, and can be planted thee to six weeks before the average last frost date.

- Moderately hardy plants handle some cold and very light frost. These can be planted two to three weeks before the average last frost date.

-Cold and frost-sensitive plants do not do well with cold weather or frost. Plant these on the average last frost date.

- Frost intolerant plants will be killed by any frost, and must be planted two to three weeks after the average last frost date. You can extend your growing season and greatly increase your yield by transplanting healthy seedlings into your garden on the recommended planting dates. Know the recommended planting dates for each plant in your garden.

WHAT TOOLS DO I NEED?

A long-handled irrigation (or round-headed) shovel is important for initial soil preparation and to remove perennial weeds and their rhizomes. A strong 12"- or 14"-wide garden rake is good for removing weeds and leveling the soil, as well as for mixing and leveling the custom-made soil in the containers.

A two-way hoe, sometimes called a scuffle or hula hoe, is best for early weeding of small weed seedlings in the aisles. It cuts them off just below the soil surface with very little movement of the soil.

Container gardens rarely require weeding. If you're watering by hand, a garden hose with a gentle watering wand will let you water quickly without washing out the custom made soil from your containers.

Plant-spacing markers save time and give your garden a professional look while providing equal light, water, and nutrition to each plant. Two rows of ½" dowels, spaced 6" and 7" apart, will help you plant most varieties properly. A wheelbarrow or large cart is useful for larger gardens.

HOW SHOULD I PLAN MY TIME?

Schedule the time to create and grow your garden. Like a cow that has to be milked twice daily, your garden needs daily care and attention to produce a high yield of healthy crops. Make a garden calendar and list the projects that need attention. That way you will not forget important things like planting dates. Plan on these time estimates for a garden of ten container beds that are each 10'-long:

- Six to eight hours to clear the area, construct containers, and make aisles.
- Four to six hours to prepare the custom soil, apply fertilizers, plant seeds, and transplant seedlings.
- Twenty minutes per day, preferably in the early morning, to water, feed, prune, and otherwise care for your plants.
- Two to ten minutes per day to harvest, depending on what and how much you are harvesting.

HOW DO I PREPARE MY GARDEN?

Clear your garden area of everything—whether living or dead—including trees, shrubs, bushes, flowers, grass, and trash. Eliminate weeds, both annual and perennial.

- Annual weeds can be plowed under or removed with a shovel, rake, or hoe.
- Perennial weeds continue growing year after year. These must be removed—roots, rhizomes (underground stems), and runners. Otherwise they will be a constant problem. Measure and stake the corners of your garden as planned. Make sure your dimensions fit the number of containers you want to have.

HELPFUL TIPS ABOUT PLANTS AND WATER

A plant is a continuous water pipe from the tip of the deepest root to the end of the tallest leaf. More than 80% of a plant's weight is water. The plant must have constant access to water at its roots.

Water keeps the plant from wilting and carries nutrients from the soil through the roots to the plant. Dry fertilizer is not useful until it's dissolved, so the nutrient compounds must be water-soluble. Plants stay cool by transpiration. Plants with a larger leaf area require more water for transpiration. Soils are not dams for storing water; therefore frequent small waterings are better than a flood once each week.

WHAT IS THE EXPECTED YIELD?

One ten-foot long container, if properly cared for, will produce about 70# to 130# of produce.

-Potatoes: 8" apart, both sides of bed, 32 plants, yield 50-100#

-Corn: 8" apart, both sides, 2 crops, 32 X 2 plants, yield 60-75 ears

With just ten 10'-long containers, or 500 square feet (just over 1/100th of an acre), your family can produce from 700# to 1,300# of fresh produce!

Short Term Food Storage for the Home

There are five methods of relatively short-term food storage: canning, freezing, drying, root cellaring, and storage of commercially packaged foods. The table below will help you to choose which method(s) of short term storage will work best for you. (Note: Freezing is the least recommended choice, due to its dependence on electricity.)

Method	Storage Life	Pros	Cons
Canning	Approx. One Year	When properly done, little risk of spoilage. Many foods may be canned. Canning gives a high-quality product similar to fresh food.	Expensive equipment. Overall, canning is a time-consuming process. There is enzyme loss due to heating. Finished product requires considerable storage space.
Freezing	Approx. 1 year for most foods (see Ball Blue Book)	Fast, easy, produces a high-quality product.	Expense of freezer. Dependence upon electricity which may not always be available. Risk of spoilage due to power failure or freezer malfunction.
Food Drying	Approx. One Year	Least expensive, most natural method. Minimal enzyme and vitamin loss. Requires little special equipment. Does not require much storage space for finished product.	Risk of insect infestation and spoilage during drying. Sometimes difficult to achieve complete, uniform drying, which is necessary to prevent spoilage. Can be a slow method to use.
Root Cellaring	Several months. Can be longer, depending upon the type of food to be stored.	After the root cellar is acquired, this is a very easy, convenient method to use.	There is always some risk of spoilage and insect and rodent infestation. Proper space for a root cellar is a prerequisite.
Prepackaged grocery items	Approx. 1 year for many items. (See table 2)	Easy, convenient. This method can be started and continued at any time. Does not require a large expenditure to begin.	You are limited to the items available in stores. Items packaged in cardboard boxes and plastic bags can be subject to insect infestation.

In canning it is stressed that one should "go by the book", i.e., *The Ball Blue Book*, or any other standard reference in canning. Although people sometimes get away with using unapproved methods (depending on the acidity if the food and other factors), to deviate from the approved methods is to invite disaster. Please don't run the risk of illness and wasted food; stick to the tried and true methods.

Storage of Prepackaged Groceries

Many grocery stores and natural food stores carry a number of nonperishable packaged food items which could be used as part of your food plan. Stockpiling these items is an easy method of food storage.

To begin, designate an area for storage. The ideal temperature is 70 degrees F or less. Temperatures higher than this will significantly reduce shelf-life. The storage area should also be one that can be kept free of insects. They can eat through cardboard and some plastic bags and infest the food. After purchasing the items, date them, then store.

As you acquire more items, rotate your stock and use the oldest items first. This method is good because you can begin by simply picking up a few extra items whenever you shop. You need to pay only a little at a time to build your supply. By stocking up on special sale items, you can cut the cost even more. Some stores offer a discount for buying by the case.

ESTIMATED SHELF LIFE OF COMERCIALLY PACKAGED FOODS

Item	Estimated Shelf Life (in months)
Dried Peas and Beans	18
Pasta	12
Salt	Indefinitely
Powdered Milk	6
Sunflower Seeds	12
Oatmeal	12
Vegetable Oil	12
Baking Soda	12
Canned Tomato Juice	6
Canned Fruit	18
Canned Vegetables	18
Canned Peanuts	18
Black Pepper	24
Raisins	12
Garlic Salt	24
Onion Salt	24
Parsley Flakes	24
Vinegar	18
Honey	18
Popcorn	24
Peanut Butter	18

Please note the following precautions:

- Never eat canned food if the seams of the can are rusty or the ends of the can are bulging out.

- Do not eat canned food that has an unusual odor.

- The contents of any can should be completely emptied as soon as the can is opened. Otherwise, in the presence of oxygen, acids from the food mix with the lead from the seams of the can, and may contaminate the food with lead.

Long Term Food Storage for the Home

The goal of long term food storage is to store basic foods that will maintain their quality and be free of infestation for five years or longer. Knowledge needed to begin such a program includes what to store, how to store it, how to keep an efficient rotation and inventory record, and what to do if infestation is noted.

The choice of foods for storage depends on availability, nutritive value, cost, storage qualities and other considerations. Store the highest quality or grade of food obtainable. For example wheat should be cereal grade, double cleaned, at least 11 percent protein and no more than 10 percent moisture.

Store foods the family is willing to eat. In times of stress it may be difficult to eat unfamiliar or disliked foods.

Below is a list of suggested basic goods for a long term storage program and the suggested quantities to store per person/per year.

BARE-MINIMUM

LDS Church Food storage requirements for 1 adult male for 1 year is approximately 2,300 calories per day (only 695lbs total).

This will keep you fed, but leave you hungry.

TOTAL FOOD PER DAY = 24.65 Ounces

-Grains (400lbs) Unless your family already eats 100% whole wheat homemade bread, white flour should be used in the transition process to whole wheat. Adding rye flour (10%) helps make wheat bread a more complete protein. Dent corn is used to make tortillas.

-Beans & Legumes (90lbs) {minimum reduced to only 60lbs in 2002} Black beans cook quickly, make a good salad complement with a vinaigrette dressing over them. Soybeans can be used to make soy milk and tofu, a protein food you should be prepared tomake. Familiarize yourself with sprouting techniques. Learn how to make wheat grass juice - the best vitamin supplement you can use.

-Milk-Dairy products (75lbs) {minimum reduced to only 16lbs in 2002} Milk powder can be used to make cottage cheese, cream cheese and hard cheeses. Ideally your milk should be fortified with Vitamins A & D. When reconstituting aerate to improve flavor (special mixing pitchers can accomplish this). Whole eggs are the best all-purpose egg product. Powdered sour cream has a limited shelf life unless frozen.

-Meats / Meat substitute (20lbs) {minimum reduced to only 0lbs in 2002} Use meat in soups, stews and beans for flavor. Freeze dried is the best option for real meat. Textured Vegetable protein is the main alternative to freeze dried meats.

-Fats / Oils (20lbs) This group can boost the calories one is getting from food storage products, and supply essential fatty acids.

-Sugars (60lbs) Store your honey in 5 gallon pails. Candy and other sweets can help with appetite fatigue.

-Fruits / Vegetables (90lbs) {minimum reduced to only zero lbs in 2002} Some fruits and vegetables are best dehydrated, others freeze dried (strawberries & blueberries). Fruits are a nice addition to hot cereal, muffins, pancakes and breads.

-Auxiliary foods (weight varies) Vanilla extract improves the flavor of powdered milk. The production of tofu requires a precipitator such as nigari, epsom salt, calcium chloride or calcium sulfide (good calcium source). Learn how to make and use wheat gluten (liquid smoke adds good flavor). Chocolate syrup and powdered drink mixes help with appetite fatigue. Vitamins and protein powders will boost the nutrition levels of foods that may have suffered losses during processing.

Note: For an average adult Female - multiply the suggested quantity by 0.75 For children ages 1-3 multiply by 0.3, 4-6 multiply by 0.5, 7-9 multiply by 0.75 For adults engaged in manual labor multiply by 1.25-1.50

For longer-term needs, and where permitted, gradually build a supply of food that will last a long time and that you can use to stay alive, such as wheat, white rice, and beans. These items can last 30 years or more when properly packaged and stored in a cool, dry place. A portion of these items may be rotated in your three-month supply.

Properly packaged, low-moisture foods stored at room temperature or cooler (75°F/24°C or lower) remain nutritious and edible much longer than previously thought according to findings of recent scientific studies. Estimated shelf life for many products has increased to 30 years or more. Previous estimates of longevity were based on "best-if-used-by" recommendations and experience. Though not studied, sugar, salt, baking soda (essential for soaking beans), and vitamin C in tablet form also store well long-term. Some basic foods do need more frequent rotation, such as vegetable oil every 1 to 2 years.

While there is a decline in nutritional quality and taste over time, depending on the original quality of food and how it was processed, packaged, and stored, the studies show that even after being stored long-term, the food will help sustain life in an emergency.

New "Life Sustaining" Shelf-Life Estimates (In Years):

Wheat 30+ White rice 30+

Corn 30+ Sugar 30+

Pinto beans 30 Rolled oats 30

Pasta 30 Potato flakes 30

Non-fat powdered milk 20

Dehydrated carrots 20

Packaging Recommendations

Recommended containers for longer-term storage include the following:

-**# 10 cans**(available at Church home storage centers)

-**Foil pouches**(available through Church Distribution Services)

-**PETE bottles**(for dry products such as wheat, corn, and beans)

These containers, used with oxygen absorber packets, eliminate food-borne insects and help preserve nutritional quality and taste. Oxygen absorber packets are available at Church home storage centers or through Church Distribution Services.

-**Plastic Buckets** Under certain conditions, you can also use plastic buckets for longer-term storage of wheat, dry beans, and other dry products.

-**Glass Jars (Canning Jars)** Under certain conditions, you may also use glass jars and lids that provide an airtight seal for longer-term storage of dry products.

Warning: Botulism poisoning may result if moist products are stored in packaging that reduces oxygen. When stored in airtight containers with oxygen absorbers, products must be dry (about 10% or less moisture content).

#10 Cans for Longer-Term Storage

#10 cans and oxygen absorbers are for sale to Church members at home storage centers. Canning sealers are available for use in the centers. Portable canning sealers may be borrowed by those wishing to do canning elsewhere.

What types of food can be packaged in the cans?

#10 cans may be used to store foods that are dry (about 10% moisture or less), shelf-stable, and low in oil content. Visit the Family Home Storage section of ProvidentLiving.org for product and storage recommendations. Many items can be stored for 20 to 30+ years. Botulism poisoning may result if moist products are stored in sealed, unprocessed cans.

How much will each can hold?

Fill volume of a #10 can is approximately .82 gallon. The weight varies by product. For example, a #10 can holds 5.8 pounds (2.6 kg) of wheat, 5.7 pounds (2.6 kg) of white rice, or 4.1 pounds (2.3 kg) of nonfat, instant dry milk.

Do foods react with the metal in the can?

No. Foods do not come in contact with the metal because they are separated from it by the can's food-grade enamel lining. The low moisture and oil content of the foods limits degradation of the can lining.

What is the best way to seal the cans?

Home storage centers have can sealers for members to use for packaging products that are available at the centers. Additionally, they have portable sealers that can be checked out by members for home or local use. Some stakes, wards, and families own portable can sealers.

Where can I find a can sealer to purchase?

Sources of #10 can sealers may be found online. Some can sealers, particularly those that do not have a motor-powered chuck, are designed for laboratory use and are not durable enough for more than incidental use. The source used by Welfare Services for a durable, portable sealer is Gering and Son in Nampa, Idaho. The Gering sealers and replacement parts are available for purchase at www.geringandson.com.

Is it necessary to use oxygen absorbers when packaging into #10 cans?

Yes, in all products except sugar. Visit providentliving.org for more information on oxygen absorber packets. The absorbers, along with a good seal, prevent insect infestation and help preserve product quality. Oxygen absorbers are available to members at home storage centers or may be ordered from ldscatalog.com and other online suppliers.

How should cans of food be stored?

The cans should be protected from moisture to prevent rust. They store best in a cool (75°F/ 24°C or lower), dry area where they are not in direct contact with floors or walls. The cans are very durable. Cases of cans may be stacked or placed under beds or in closets.

Are #10 cans a packaging option for emergency kits?

No. Many emergency kit items are not suitable for packaging in cans. First aid items and food rations, such as granola bars, are best stored in containers with removable lids to allow for frequent rotation.

Where can I find #10 cans?

Cans are available for members to purchase at home storage centers. Refer to Home Storage Centers on ProvidentLiving.org for a list of locations. Other supply options include online resources, local commercial canneries, or container suppliers (check the yellow pages under headings such as "cans," "containers," or similar listings).

Foil Pouches for Longer-Term Storage

What type of pouch is available at home storage centers, at Distribution Services, and online at ldscatalog.com?

The pouches are made of multilayer laminated plastic and aluminum. Thematerial is 7 mils thick (178 microns) and protects food against moisture and insects.

What are other sources for foil pouches?

There are a variety of sources for foil pouches (commonly referred to as Mylar bags). Foil pouches available at home storage centers, at Distribution Services, and online at ldscatalog.com are by far the most economical choice, but come in only one size, which is discussed below. Other sizes and suppliers can be found many different places on the internet. One that seems to have the most variety and best prices is www.sorbentsystems.com/mylar.html.

What types of foods can be packaged in pouches?

The pouches can be used to store foods that are dry (about 10% moisture or less), shelf-stable, and low in oil content. Botulism poisoning may result if moist products are stored in oxygen reduced packaging. Visit providentliving.org for specific product recommendations.

How much food does each pouch hold?

Each pouch holds 1 gallon (4 liters) of product. The weight varies by product. A pouch holds 7 pounds (3.2 kg) of wheat, 6.8 pounds (3.1 kg) of white rice, or 5 pounds (2.3 kg) of dry milk.

Do foods react with the aluminum in the pouch?

No. Foods do not come in contact with the aluminum because they are separated from it by a layer of food-grade plastic. The metal barrier is important in protecting the food from moisture and oxygen.

What is the best way to seal pouches?

Pouches should be sealed using an impulse sealer (see related instructions). Some use an iron or another household heating device to seal, but this method may not provide an adequate seal, especially for powdered products such as flour or dry milk. The impulse sealers used by Welfare Services (American International Electric AIE 305 A1 and Mercier ME 305 A1) meet the following specifications: 3/16-inch (5 mm) wide seal, 11.5-inch (305 mm) wide jaws, rated for up to 8-mil (205microns) thick pouches, and equipped with a safety switch to cancel operation if the jaw is obstructed.

Where can I find an impulse sealer?

Impulse sealers are available at most home storage centers. Many stakes also have impulse sealers available. If you prefer, you may purchase an impulse sealer from Distribution Services or online at ldscatalog.com.

Is it necessary to remove all the air from the pouches?

No. Oxygen absorbers remove only the oxygen from the air in the pouches. The low oxygen content eliminates food-borne insects and helps preserve product quality. Visit providentliving.org for additional information on oxygen absorbers.

Is it normal for the sides of the pouch to pull in once the pouch is sealed?

With most products, the sides of sealed pouches will pull in slightly within a few days of packaging. This is more noticeable with granular foods than with powdered products. Visit providentliving.org for additional information on oxygen absorbers.

How should pouches of food be stored?

The pouches store best in a cool, dry, rodent-free area. Storage containers should not be in direct contact with concrete floors or walls.

Are pouches rodent proof?

Pouches are not rodent proof. If rodents or other pests are a significant potential problem in the storage area, the pouches should be placed into containers that are rodent or pest proof. Do not store them in containers that have been used to store nonfood items.

Should emergency kits be packaged in pouches?

Many emergency supply items are not suitable for packaging in foil pouches. First aid items and food rations, such as granola bars, are best stored in containers with removable lids to allow for frequent rotation.

PETE Bottles for Longer-Term Storage

Bottles made of PETE (polyethylene terephthalate) plastic can be used with oxygen absorbers to store products such as wheat, corn, and dry beans. PETE bottles are identified on the container with the letters PETE or PET under the recycle symbol

Other types of plastic bottles typically do not provide an adequate moisture or oxygen barrier for use with oxygen absorbers. Do not use containers that were previously used to store nonfood items. PETE bottles can also be used for shorter-term storage (up to 5 years) of other shelf-stable dry foods such as white rice. Visit providentliving.org for specific product recommendations. Moisture content of stored foods should be about 10 percent or less. When moist products are stored in reduced oxygen packaging, botulism poisoning may occur.

Packaging in PETE Bottles

1. Use PETE bottles that have screw-on lids with plastic or rubber lid seals. You can verify that the lid seal will not leak by placing a sealed empty bottle under water and pressing on it. If you see bubbles escape from the bottle, it will leak.

2. Clean used bottles with dish soap, and rinse them thoroughly to remove any residue. Drain out the water, and allow the bottles to dry completely before you use them for packaging food products.

3. Place an oxygen absorber in each bottle. The absorbers can be used with containers of up to one gallon capacity (4 liters). Additional instruction about using oxygen absorbers is available at providentliving.org.

4. Fill bottles with wheat, corn, or dry beans.

5. Wipe top sealing edge of each bottle clean with a dry cloth and screw lid on tightly.

6. Store the products in a cool, dry location, away from light.

7. Protect the stored products from rodents.

8. Use a new oxygen absorber each time you refill a bottle for storage.

Where to Get Oxygen Absorber Packets

Oxygen absorber packets are available at home storage centers and Church Distribution Services, or they can be ordered online at ldscatalog.com. Unused oxygen absorbers can be stored in glass jars with metal lids that have gaskets.

Plastic Buckets for Longer-Term Storage

Plastic buckets may be used to store food commodities that are dry (about 10 percent moisture or less) and low in oil content. Only buckets made of food-grade plastic with gaskets in the lid seals should be used. Buckets that have held nonfood items should not be used. To prevent insect infestation, dry ice (frozen carbon dioxide) should be used to treat grains and dry beans stored in plastic buckets. Treatment methods that depend on the absence of oxygen to kill insects, such as oxygen absorbers or nitrogen gas flushing, are not effective in plastic buckets. Avoid exposing food to humid, damp conditions when packaging them.

Dry Ice Treatment Instructions

1. Use approximately one ounce of dry ice per gallon (7 grams per liter) capacity of the container. Do not use dry ice in metal containers of any kind or size because of the potential for inadequate seals or excessive buildup of pressure.

2. Wear gloves when handling dry ice.

3. Wipe frost crystals from the dry ice, using a clean dry towel.

4. Place the dry ice in the center of the container bottom.

5. Pour the grain or dry beans on top of the dry ice. Fill the bucket to within one inch (25mm) of the top.

6. Place the lid on top of the container and snap it down only about halfway around the container. The partially sealed lid will allow the carbon dioxide gas to escape from the bucket as the dry ice sublimates (changes from a solid to a gas).

7. Allow the dry ice to sublimate completely before sealing the bucket. Feel the bottom of the container to see if the dry ice is all gone. If the bottom of the container is very cold, dry ice is still present.

8. Monitor the bucket for a few minutes after sealing the lid. If the bucket or lid bulges, slightly lift the edge of the lid to relieve pressure.

9. It is normal for the lid of the bucket to pull down slightly as a result of the partial vacuum caused when carbon dioxide is absorbed into the product.

Storage of Plastic Buckets

Store plastic buckets off the floor by at least ½ inch (1.3 cm) to allow air to circulate under the bucket. Do not stack plastic buckets over three high. If buckets are stacked, check them periodically to ensure that the lids have not broken from the weight.

Visit providentliving.org for additional information.

Glass Jars for Longer-Term Storage

A chemical free, oxygen free process which is recommended for safe food storage is vacuum sealing in glass jars with airtight lids. There are several products available that you can vacuum seal longer term storage in glass jars at home.

Pump-n-Seal, an inexpensive hand-powered vacuum sealer, which can be used with either new or used jars, provided the jars have a rubber ring on the inside surface. (Peanut butter and other commonly available foods come in such jars, giving one the opportunity to recycle.)

(Note: Some have successfully used the Pump-n-Seal to store a variety of foods, but have sometimes encountered one problem. The small plastic strips one uses on the lids were sometimes chewed up by mice, thus breaking the vacuum seal. This can be solved this by using the Pump-n-Seal in the usual way, then covering the plastic strip and the area around it on the jar lid with aluminum heat-duct tape from the hardware store.) For more information visit www.pump-n-seal.com.

Vacuum Food Sealers

Vacuum food storage systems like the Food Saver have options and attachments that allow you to seal products in your existing glass jars. The FoodSaver® Wide-Mouth Jar Sealer fits on your own Ball® and Kerr®Mason jars and works with FoodSaver® Vacuum Sealer Systems to keep foods fresh longer. For more information visit www.foodsaver.com. Also see an excellent instructional video on this process at http://www.youtube.com/watch?v=ISKgIOqP5xA, or Google *Foodsaver Jars*.

If using glass jars it is best to replace them in the box in which they were bought to omit light, help protect them from breakage and for convenience in handling and storage. The outside of the box should be marked with the contents and the date, the notation facing outward for easy inventory.

Approved Dry Pack Products

Dry-pack products for home storage need to be low moisture (10% moisture or less), good quality, and insect free. Packaging in foil pouches, #10 cans, glass canning jars, and PETE plastic bottles should be limited to foods that best retain flavor and nutritional value. An oxygen absorber packet should be included in each container for all products except sugar.

APPROVED PRODUCTS

- Milk Non-fat dry milk and milk/whey products such as hot cocoa
- White Flour Bleached or unbleached
- Whole Grains Wheat, white rice, dry corn, popcorn, rye, barley, etc. Grains that are not milled or cracked and do not have an oily seed coat
- Rolled Oats Quick or regular
- Legumes Dry peas and beans, including dehydrated refried beans
- Pasta products that do not contain egg
- Fruits and Dehydrated or freeze-dried products that are dry enough to snap. Vegetables (Best items: apples, bananas, potatoes, onions, carrots, corn, and peas. Marginal items: apricots, peaches, pears, tomatoes, and green beans)

- Sugar Granulated or powdered (Do not use oxygen absorbers in containers of sugar)
- Miscellaneous TVP (Texturized vegetable protein), Cheese powder, Gelatin, Soup mixes (without bouillon)

NON-APPROVED PRODUCTS

The following items are examples of products that do not store well due to high moisture or oil content. These items keep best when stored in freezer bags in a freezer:

- Milled Grain Whole wheat flour, Cornmeal, Cereal, Granola
- Oily Grain/Seeds Nuts, Brown rice, Pearled barley, Sesame

The following types of products should be stored in their original containers and rotated frequently:

- Leavening Includes mixes containing leavening such as cake or biscuit mix
- Miscellaneous Spices, Oil, Bouillon, Dried Meat, Dried Eggs, Brown Sugar, Candy, First-aid supplies NOTE: All food items should be rotated. This may be accomplished by personal use or by sharing with others.

Your Long-Term Storage Area

The storage area should be clean and away from heating units and damp areas. The bottom shelf should be 2-3 feet above the ground in flood prone areas. A 9ft x 12ft room with ten foot ceilings will provide adequate space for a family of six to store eighteen months' worth of food. Utilize a space where it would be difficult for insects and rodents to find harborage. Good housekeeping is an important factor to help prevent infestation.

Typical places in the home that are usually easily adapted for long term storage areas are basements, pantries, back halls, enclosed porches or breezeways, sheds, and bulk-heads. Closets, attics, space under beds, an unused room, stairways or space made available by family or friends can be used. An inventory and rotation schedule should be maintained on the stored food. The inventory should be done monthly to:

1. Check bulk grains for rodent and insect infestation
2. Make sure the food is being rotated properly

3. Remove bulged cans or unsealed packages

4. Make sure the written inventory is accurately kept

5. Check the temperature of the room throughout the year to maintain proper storage temperatures. When checking for infestation it is only necessary to check one or two containers from each lot. If contamination is evident, the rest of the lot should be checked. To deal with infested food, small quantities of grain.(1-10 pounds) can be put in medium to heavy grade plastic bags and placed in the deep freeze for 2-3 days. This will usually destroy all stages of any insects which may be present. Insect fragments may be re-moved by pouring the dry food through a stream of fan air into another container. Then process the food again for storage but place in the front of the storage area to be used first. For more specific information regarding appropriate foods and optimal storage conditions consult local universities or government agencies, or visit www.providentliving.org.

Successful food storage depends on several factors:

- Quality of products - obtain top grade food products when possible

- Proper Containers - use heavy plastic, metal or glass with tight fitting lids

- Storage areas - easy access, dark, cool, dry, free from rodents insects/other pests

- Temperature - food stores best at 40-60 F

- Variety - provides better nutrition and avoids appetite fatigue

- Rotation - date and rotate to minimize loss of food value and flavor, prevent spoilage

- Inventory - Maintain a record of items used and added

Wheat Grinder Basics

For most families, especially for the families in our area of the country, the majority of our long term food storage will consist mainly of wheat in the raw form. In this form, the uses of the wheat is somewhat limited. Therefore, a family should have the ability to process the wheat into a more useful form. The easiest way to do this is a basic wheat grinder. The three types of commonly available wheat grinders are discussed below.

Stone Grinders

Stone Grinders are the oldest type of grinder there is. Stone grinders have two circular grinding stones. One stone turns against a stationary stone. When grain is ground, it falls through a channel into the center of the two stones. As the stone rotates, it pulls the grain out through the channels where it is ground. The flour falls out the outer edges of the two stones.

Favorable Characteristics

-Very durable -Adjustable to any setting from cracked wheat to fine flour -Can grind grain that has not been completely cleaned -Should last a lifetime

Unfavorable Characteristics

- Usually larger, bulkier machines -Grind more slowly than impact grinders -Stones quickly become 'loaded' if you grind oil bearing seeds or nuts

-Higher heat of grind can cause a loss of nutrients

-Grit in Flour

Burr Grinders

Burr grinders are nearly identical to stone grinders except their grinding wheels are made out of steel with small burrs protruding out the sides (sometimes called "teeth") which shear the grain into flour. Burr grinders have some advantages and disadvantages over stone grinders.

Favorable Characteristics

-Will grind dry grains as well as oil bearing seeds

-Can be either powered or hand crank operated.

-Adjustable to any setting from cracked wheat to fine flour

-Burrs are easily replaceable

Unfavorable Characteristics

-Will not grind as finely as a stone grinder. (But close!) -Grind more slowly than impact grinders

Impact Grinders

Impact grinders use rows of 'blades' placed in circular rows on metal wheels. One wheel turns and the other wheel is stationary, like the stone grinder. The rotating wheel turns at several thousand RPM. As grain is fed into the center of the fixed wheel, the interaction between the two wheels 'impacts' the grain and pulverizes it into fine flour as the grain works its way to the outside of the wheels.

Favorable Characteristics

-Very small, light and compact -Can be put in the cupboard when not in use -Grinds very quickly - Grinds grain into very fine flour

Unfavorable Characteristics

-The blades are somewhat fragile. Small rocks or metal pieces will damage and misalign the wheels.

-Can be very noisy -Even on the coarsest setting the flour comes out relatively fine. No Hand crank operation, only electric operation

Popular Wheat Grinders

Nutrimill Grain Mill The Nutrimill is the first high speed stoneless flour mill with multitexture grinding. It's the perfect way to make flour. The Nutrimill uses TruGrind milling heads to mill grain into flour. There are no stones in this mill thus reducing heat and increasing the speed of grinding. The Nutrimill incorporates a variable drive motor that lets you achieve the texture that you want for your baking needs. The Nutrimill is a dependable multifunction grain mill with a lifetime warranty.

Impact Grinder **MSRP $270**

WonderMill (Formerly The Whisper Mill) High speed, stainless steel mill will not overheat your flour, preserving the grain's natural vitamins. Control knob allows setting fine to coarse milling, throughput is nearly 100 pounds per hour. Maintenance and trouble free design - no gumming, jamming or glazing, unlike other mills. 12-cup capacity flour receiver doubles as a convenient storage canister. 1-3/4 hp motor, 120 volts. For household use only. Limited lifetime warranty.

Impact Grinder **MSRP $260**

The Family Grain Mill is unique in that it offers grain mill, flaker mill, and several other attachments, as well as a choice of hand powered, electric, or both. But with the Family Grain Mill you can have the convenience of an electric mill without giving up the utility and practicality of a mill that doesn't depend on electricity. The Family Grain Mill is the least expensive mill we've seen that actually works well, grinds reasonably fine, and is reasonably fast. Made in Germany. Lifetime limited warranty from the importer

Burr Grinder **MSRP $130**

K-Tec / BlendTec Kitchen Mill Wheat Grinder Instead of stones, The Kitchen Mill™ uses a computer-balanced Micronetic Chamber to grind grain into flour. This type chamber is used in the pharmaceutical industry to create exact uniform particles for medicines. K-TEC made history by being the first manufacturer to bring the dependability of micronetics into the home for kitchen use.

Impact Grinder **MSRP $180**

Wolfgang Grain Mill The German-engineered Wolfgang is a Grain Mill without compromise. It can effortlessly grind 3.5 ounces of grain in the finest flour every minute. Its extremely hard ceramic/corundum millstones and strong industrial motor ensure maximum performance for years to come. It is made in Germany with solid Beechwood cabinetry, yet is still the affordable way to provide nutrition to your loved ones.

Stone Grinder **MSRP $500**

The Country Living Grain Mill is made in the USA and built like the proverbial "tank." Quality is outstanding, from its stout cast metal housing and sealed ball bearings to its huge 5" precision steel burr plates and robust handle and flywheel. Turning effort is very easy for a hand operated mill, producing a cup of wheat flour in about 1-1/4 minutes.

Burr Grinder **MSRP $400**

Some delicious wheat recipes

Kathy's Bread

- 4 cups warm water -3 TBSP yeast -½ tsp sugar Dissolve Together

-1 cup eggs (4 or 5) -1 cube blue bonnet margarine

-1 cup honey combine and add

-16 cups flour (up to ½ wheat) - 4 tsp salt add and mix well

Let rise in warm oven until double. Form into 6 loaves and let rise again for 30 min. in warm oven. Place in preheated oven (350 degrees) and cook for 22 min or until golden brown. Makes 6 loaves. You may substitute some flour for a 7 grain mix.

Wheat Salad

1 ½ cups of wheat. Soak the wheat overnight and then cook 2 hours or until soft. Cool well.

-8 oz. Cream Cheese softened -1 large Cool Whip

-1-15 oz can of crushed pineapple

-2 small pkgs instant vanilla pudding -3 Tbsp. Lemon juice -½ cup walnuts chopped Sprinkle vanilla pudding over softened cream cheese, stir in lemon juice, pineapple. Fold in Cool Whip. Add Wheat. Refrigerate till set.

Wheat Chili

-3 Cups Wheat - 6 Cups Water - 6 Bullion cubes Soak overnight. Cook over medium heat 1 hr.

-1 Lb. Ground beef -1 tsp salt -¼ tsp garlic powder

-1 Cup chopped green peppers -1 Cup chopped onions - 1/8 tsp oregano -1/8 tsp cumin

-1 can tomatoes -1/8 tsp paprika -1 can tomato sauce (or 3 TBSP paste) -Dash of cayenne pepper

-1 TBSP chili powder

sauté meat with spices until brown. Add tomatoes and simmer 15 min. add to the wheat, plus the tomato sauce. Simmer until wheat is tender, about 1 hr. or more. Enjoy!

Water Storage

Principles of Water Storage

Store drinking water for circumstances in which the water supply may be polluted or disrupted. If water comes directly from a good, pretreated source, then no additional purification is needed; otherwise, pretreat water before use. Store water in sturdy, leakproof, breakage-resistant containers. Consider using plastic bottles commonly used for juices and soft drinks. Keep water containers away from heat sources and direct sunlight. Water versus Food-You can last on average about two to three weeks without food, but only about three days without water. (This is a rough estimate; there are a lot of influencing factors that would increase or decrease these numbers.) Often Neglected- It is estimated that no more than 5% of families have more than two weeks of water storage in their home. Water is one of the most important storage items, yet for whatever reason is often neglected.

Problems of water storage

Size-Water storage consumes a great deal of space. A typical 55 gallon drum is about two feet wide by three feet tall. Not everybody has an unfinished basement or garage with sufficient space to store multiple barrels or other containers Storage-Water may be stored in a variety of containers. Some containers and storage locations adversely affect the water supply by leeching chemicals into the water or affecting the taste. Additionally, some containers may degrade or disintegrate with time, leaking your water into the surrounding area.

Contaminants- It is hard to know with accuracy the history of the water you are drinking. Where has it been, what has it been treated with, and how long has it been sitting still? What temperatures has it been subjected to, how much sunlight exposure has it had, and for how long? Poor conditions such as those listed above create opportunities for unwanted bacteria and organisms to grow in your water supply.

Purification-There are a variety of suggestions on how best to purify water, many of them conflicting with each other.

Practices of water storage

Water should only be stored in food-grade plastic or other material that is created specifically for long term storage of liquids intended for consumption. It is important that you be careful what you store your water in, as some containers can leech, crack, degrade, or otherwise cause problems with your water. Before storing your water, it is usually a good idea to wash and sanitize the container. This can be done by mixing 1 teaspoon (5 ml) of liquid household chlorine bleach to one quart (1 liter) of water. Do not use bleach that has scents, additives, or thickeners. It is not necessary to treat water that is already chlorinated before storing it. Many cities chlorinate their water supply, so if that's the case in your city, any water from your tap is safe and ready to be stored in an appropriate container without any extra action on your part. Exposure to light plays a large part in the development of bacteria; where possible, it's best to store your water in a cool, dark place (same goes for your food). The following are a few of the more popular methods for storing water.

Water Storage

The following are many different methods in storing water within your home. Eash method has it's pros and cons and you may want to determine which method will work best for you and your storage situation.

55 gallon water drums

55 gallon drums of water are a popular choice for home storage. For new drums, try the oft-recurring Maceys preparedness sales where you can find them for about $40. You can buy used drums much cheaper, though these often have contained syrups and other things that need to be sufficiently washed out before usage. Water stored in barrels should ideally be rotated once yearly, but you can get away with storing it for a few years and purifying it before drinking.

Pros:

- Dark blue plastic restricts light, thus helping prevent bacteria and algae growth

- Some drums/barrels can be stacked to maximize space

Cons:

- Difficult to move once filled

- Siphon/pump must be used to retrieve water from top of the barrel (working against gravity) (Cost per gallon: $0.73 assuming $40 for a new barrel)

5 gallon boxes

5 gallon water boxes are a good choice for putting water storage in random, small spaces. Boxes should not be stacked more than three high. Water is stored inside the box in a metallic bag. Emergency Essentials (www.beprepared.com) sells 5 boxes (so 25 gallons total) for $33 Water kept in these boxes should last a few years; rotation once every three to four years is a good idea.

Pros:

- Easy to move once filled (each 5 gallon box weighs ~40 pounds when full)

- Box can be reused after water is consumed. (Emergency Essentials says you can use the box as a toilet - have fun!)

- Easy dispensing spout to retrieve water when desired

Cons:

- Material is not too durable (Cost per gallon: $1.32 assuming $33 for 5 5-gallon boxes)

-

250+ gallon water tanks

For the ambitious, you can acquire industrial-type water tanks that store 250+ gallons, commonly known as an IBC (Intermediate Bulk Container). These food-grade plastic bladders are housed in a metal cage and can be stacked two or three high. Remember: water weighs eight pounds per gallon, so 250 pounds of water is 2,000 pounds, plus about 150 pounds for the cage. Make sure your flooring can support this weight! Rotate water stored in these tanks once yearly.

Pros:

- Water spigot is at the bottom, so you can use gravity to get the water out

- Stackable, so you can fit a year supply of water in your garage or basement

- With an adapter you can connect a garden hose

Cons:

- Pretty much impossible to move once full (Cost per gallon: $1.64 assuming $450 for 275 gallon tank)

1 gallon jug

You can buy one gallon jugs at any supermarket These are usually very cheap (~$0.70 per jug) and an affordable way to get some basic water storage going. These bottles are not a good solution for long term storage, as they will degrade within a year and leak all of their contents. Harder plastic (like 2 liter soda bottles) is a better solution.

Pros:

- Inexpensive and easy to buy a few at a time with your normal grocery purchases
- Small container is easy to store under furniture, on closet shelves, and other small places

Cons:

- Plastic container degrades after about a year and will leak
- For long term storage, chemicals from the plastic may leech into water

(Cost per gallon: $0.70 assuming $0.70 for 1 gallon jug)

Hard plastic water jugs

There are several types of water jugs that have harder plastic, making them more durable for longer term storage. Some water companies sell pre-bottled jugs that you can simply buy and store. Another option is to buy empty, hard plastic jugs (such as the one pictured above) and fill it yourself. Either way, these jugs will last a lot longer than the ones in the previous column, making them a smarter (though costlier) option for small amounts of water storage. Water stored in these jugs can be easily rotated (use them to water plants, for example), so try to cycle them every six months.

Pros:

- Durable, heavier plastic will last longer than other types of jugs
- Easy to move, rotate, or stack on top of one another

Cons:

- Expensive option for small amounts of water storage

(Cost per gallon: $2.20 assuming $11 for 5 gallon jug)

4.2 ounce water pouch

Emergency water pouches are a good item for your 72 hour kits, but should not be used for home storage.

Pros:

- Lasts up to five years
- Easy way to store small amounts of water in 72 hour kits, backpacks, cars, and other locations

Cons:

- Inefficient method of storing a large amount of water

(Cost per gallon: $9.45 assuming $0.31 for 4.2 oz. pouch)

PURIFICATION

Depending on how you have stored your water and how long it's been sitting in its container, it will be necessary to purify it before it is used. There are a variety of methods out there, and lots of information that is difficult at times to sift through. It is important that you review the possible purification methods, and decide what works for you. Please note that water storage, like any emergency preparedness, should have various contingency plans in place. Your desired method of purification might be to boil the water, but if you have no fuel, you'll need a Plan B. Thus, it's usually a good idea to prioritize the three methods you would like to use, and then acquire the necessary supplies or skills that will allow you to purify in each method.

It's also not a bad idea to double up on purification, just to be sure. For example, you may sift your water through a particle filter (such as a coffee filter) to remove any debris, add some iodine drops to the water, and then pass it through a carbon filter. Better safe than sorry!

The following are a few of the more popular purification methods.

Bleach

Disinfecting with household bleach kills some, but not all, types of disease-causing organisms. The bleach must contain chlorine in order to work. Do not use scented bleaches, color-safe bleaches, or bleaches with added cleaners. Most household chlorine bleaches have 4-6% available chlorine, in which case you should add 1/8 teaspoon (8 drops) of regular, unscented, liquid household bleach for each gallon of water (2 drops per quart/liter), stir it well, cover, and let it stand for 30 minutes before you use it. Double the amount of chlorine if the water is cloudy, murky, or colored, or if the water is extremely cold. If after sitting covered for 30 minutes the water doesn't have a slight chlorine odor, repeat the dosage and let sit for another 15 minutes. Most of the chlorine content in bleach will evaporate within a year, so this is not a good long-term storage item.

Iodine (drops/tablets)

Disinfecting with iodine is generally less effective than chlorine in controlling the parasite Giardia, but it's better than no treatment at all. Add 5 drops of 2% iodine (from the medicine chest or first aid kit) to every quart/liter of clear water; add 10 drops if the water is cloudy. Let the solution stand for at least 30 minutes. For commercially prepared chlorine or iodine tablets, follow the instructions that come with them. If you don't have instructions, use one tablet for each quart/liter of water to be purified.

SODIS (Solar Disinfection)

Solar water disinfection is a simple method to improve the quality of drinking water by using sunlight to inactivate pathogens causing diarrhea. Contaminated water is filled into transparent plastic bottles and exposed to the full sunlight for 6 hours. During the exposure, the UV-A radiation of the sunlight destroys the pathogens. SODIS does not change the chemical water quality. It requires relatively clear water to work, and is ineffective with large amounts of water. More information on this technique is available at http://www.sodis.ch/

Gravity carbon filters

Gravity-based systems are very effective in removing contaminants from water because of the extremely long "contact period." Some of the other filtration systems rely on water pressure that forces water molecules through the filters at 60-90 PSI. In such systems, individual water molecules come in contact with the filter media for a mere fraction of a second. Water molecules passing through the ceramic purification elements in these filters are drawn gently by gravity and stay in contact with the media for several minutes. You can filter water in these units for around two cents per gallon, and they are great and removing dangerous organisms such as protozoan cysts (Cryptosporidium, Giardia, etc.) and microscopic bacteria (E. coli, Salmonella, etc.). The two leading brands of these types of filters are the Aquarain (http://www.aquarain.com/) and Berkey (http://www.berkeyfilters.com/) units.

Chlorine

Chlorinating concentrate can be found at your local pool/spa store, and can be used to purify your water. This product is a granulated powder. The powder can last a lot longer than its corresponding (and diluted) liquid form, so you should store the powder until you are ready to use it. You must be sure that the active ingredient of the product you're purchasing is 97-99% Sodium dichloro-s-triazinetrione dihydrate. Several chlorine products have other additives that should not be used, so make sure that you check the label.

To use, mix 1/4 of a teaspoon into 55 gallons of water. Close the lid, wait 24 hours. Open lid - if you don't smell chlorine, repeat the previous step. When you smell chlorine, leave lid off and let chlorine gas escape until there is no smell. It is ready for use when the smell is gone. Be careful how you store the powder; where possible, it's best to keep it in its sealed container so prevent fumes from escaping and damaging surrounding items.

Boiling

Boiling kills most types of disease-causing organisms and is the most recommended purification technique. Bring the water to a rolling boil for at least one minute, then let it cool. If you are more than one mile above sea level, boil for three minutes. Though it is important to conserve fuel, the longer you boil your water, the better chance you have at eliminating any possible organisms or bacteria. As the water cools, you can stir it once a minute to mix air into the water, which will help reduce any bad taste the water may have.

Sports bottle with filter

A recently popular preparedness item is a sports bottle with a carbon-based filter included. These bottles would allow you to filter water "on the go" in an emergency, such as from a lake, stream, or other body of water. If using a source of water that might contain extreme bacteriological or viral contamination, it is recommended that two drops of plain chlorine or iodine be added to each refill before filtering. This will kill minute pathogens such as viruses. The disinfectant will then be filtered from the water entirely, removing its odor, color and taste.

- LDS Church water storage guidelines
(http://www.providentliving.org)

- CDC information on water storage
(http:/www.bt.cdc.gov/disasters/earthquakes/food.asp)

Important non-food items for storage

Tools
Adjustable wrench/hammer & nails
Ax/Saw
Bailing Wire/Twine
Broom/dustpan
Bucket
Clothesline and clothes pins
Crowbar
Gloves (Heavy Work)
Pliers
Rope – heavy duty
Screwdrivers
Shovel
Tape (Duct/plastic/electrical)
Tarps

Cooking
Aluminum Foil (Heavy Duty & regular)
Bucket or dishpan
Canning lids/paraffin wax)
Can opener (non-electric)
Campstove & Fuel
Charcoal & lighter fluid
Dish cloth/ dish towel/scrubbie
Dish detergent
Dutch oven
Napkins/paper towels

Paper plates/cups/utensils
Plastic wrap/wax paper/zip lock bags, coffee filters
Pots/pans (at least 2)
Sharp Knife
Utensils

Bedding
Blankets/quilts (enough to keep each person warm with
no other heat source)
Pillows
Rubberized Sheets
Sheets (Flannel are warmer & more absorbent)
Sleeping bags

Clothing
Boots – extra laces
Gloves – warm and seasonal
Jacket/ Warm Coat
Poncho - Seasonal Clothing
Shoes/2 socks (at least 1 pair wool)

Safety Items
Batteries - many sizes
Candles
Flashlights
Fire Extinguisher
Garden Hose (firefighting/ siphoning gas)
Insecticides
Lantern & Fuel – extra mantels

Matches/lighters
Paper & pencils
Radio (battery operated)
2 way radios and batteries

Sanitation

Large trash can w/ tight fitting lid
Ammonia
Bleach
Clean rags
Disinfectant (Lysol, Pinesol, etc)
Newspapers (to wrap garbage & waste in, could also be used for fuel or blankets)
Plastic bags (various sizes especially garbage bags)
Toilet paper
Wet Wipes

Hygiene Supplies

Combs/brushes
Contact Lens solutions
Deodorant
Extra Glasses
Feminine Supplies
Hand soap (15 bars/person/year)
Infant Supplies (Disposable diapers, plastic pants, bottles)
Laundry detergent (25 lbs/person/year)
Shampoo/Conditioner
Shaving supplies
Tissue

Toothbrush/toothpaste
Wash Cloths/Towels

Pets
Food
Leashes/collars
Litter box supplies
Medications

Financial Preparedness

When many think of preparing for an emergency, they typically think of first aid kits, flashlights, and food storage. In the aftermath of a disaster, it's hard to imagine that money matters will be a top priority, but as things begin to settle down and get back to normal, you may find that the financial side of things is a significant source of stress and concern. The government might be there to help if the disaster is serious enough, but even if you can secure a little assistance from  Uncle Sam, this assistance typically comes in the form of loans that must be paid back (with interest). Any grants you receive would only be enough to meet immediate needs, not to repair or recover your possessions. The good news is that, as always, you can make things easier on yourself and your family by planning ahead.

Create a financial disaster recovery kit by gathering the following items together and storing them in a safe location, whether it be a home safe or a portable, waterproof bag.

Legal Documents: birth certificates, marriage licenses, divorce papers, child custody papers, passports, driver's licenses, social security cards, naturalization papers and residency documents, military/veteran's papers, powers of attorney (including healthcare powers of attorney), will or trust documents

Medical Information: records of past procedures, allergies, pre-existing conditions

Financial Documents: cash (as ATM or bank services may be disrupted), bank statements, insurance policies, credit card numbers, a list of phone numbers for financial institutions and credit card companies where you have accounts

Residential Items: an inventory of household possessions, appraisals of valuable items (jewelry, art, antiques, heirlooms), home improvement records, deeds/titles and other ownership records for property such as homes and automobiles

Critical Computer Files: multiple backup copies of important documents from your personal and work computers

Contact Information: a list of names, phone numbers, and e-mail addresses of family members, friends, business contacts, and emergency assistance agencies in your area, such as the Red Cross.

A basic four-point formula to attain and maintain financial preparedness:

1. Pay your tithes and offerings.
2. Get out of debt and stay out of debt.
3. Use your surplus funds wisely.
4. Maintain an emergency stash of money.

In getting out of debt and staying out of debt, there are certain basic principles that we, as individuals and families, can apply, such as:

- Live within your income.
- Prepare and use short- and long-term budgets.
- Regularly save a part of your income.
- Use your credit wisely, if it is necessary to use it at all. For example, a reasonable debt may be justified for the acquisition of a home or education.
- Preserve and utilize your assets through appropriate tax and estate planning.

By following these simple, basic principles it is possible to get out of debt and stay out of debt.

By keeping emergency cash, you protect yourself from life's unknowns. You've got a safety net just in case an emergency prevents you from accessing your bank accounts. You might lose your job, incur medical expenses, or have other accounts frozen in error. If any of these things should happen, you'd need money fast. Your emergency cash is there for you.

Important and Precious Documents

Family Information Record

In addition to emergency survival supplies you should also collect vital family information. Record and keep it in at least two safe places-a fire resistant "get-away" box that you can take with you if you have to leave the home, and a safe-deposit box at your bank or credit union.

The following items would be useful for you to record and keep in these two locations:

- Genealogy records
- Full name and social security numbers of all family members
- Listing of vehicles, boats etc. with identification and license numbers
- Listing of all charge account card numbers and expiration dates, bank account numbers (both checking and saving), insurance policy numbers, securities, deeds, and loan numbers showing the company name, address and telephone numbers.
- Name, address, and telephone number for each of the following:
- employer - schools
- fire/paramedics - family contacts
- utility company - police
- doctor - hospital
- attorney - civil defense
- insurance policies - deeds
- securities - licenses
- loans - will
- safe-deposit box key - vehicle titles

- birth/death certificates
- social security I.D. cards
- citizenship papers
- letter of instruction
- tax returns (last 5 years)
- Location of important documents

Some other important financial and legal documents you need to keep safe in a place where you or your heirs can get them. Sometimes a copy is not the same as the original and does not have the same validity.

-*Living Wills, *Powers of attorney and *Medical powers of attorney
-*Wills and trusts
-*Titles and Deeds
-*Birth Certificates/ *Adoption decrees/ *Naturalization Records
-*Marriage License/divorce papers and child custody papers
-Passports and military/veteran papers
-Social Security cards, Drivers License or ID cards
-Certificates for stocks, bonds, investments
-Insurance policies (life, home, auto)
-List of health and medical information
-List of financial investment information including account numbers
-Important contact information (family, friends, doctors, attorneys, ins. agents
-Household inventory documentation
-Mortgage
-Genealogy, pictures, and Family History

This information could be put on a disk, thumb drive, or CD.

*It is necessary to have the original or a certified copy.

CAUTION!!! This information must be safeguarded and protected. This information in the wrong hands would make identity theft very easy.

Emergency Heat

During severe winter storms, your home heating system could be inoperative for as long as several days. To minimize discomfort and possible health problems during this time, conserve body heat by dressing warmly; find or improvise an alternative heat source, such as a fireplace or electric space heater; confine heating to a single room; and keep safety a foremost consideration. While chances of freezing to death in your home are small, there's a greater danger of death by fire, lack of oxygen or carbon monoxide poisoning.

Think "Safety First"

Safety is critical in a heating emergency. Follow these precautions:

- Do not burn anything larger than candles inside your home without providing good ventilation to the outside.

- Any type of heater (except electric) should be vented. Connect the stove pipe to a chimney flue if at all possible. Or hook up your stove to the flue entrance of the nonfunctioning furnace pipe. If no other alternative exists, consider extending a stove pipe through a window. Replace the window glass with a metal sheet and run the temporary stove pipe through the metal.

- If you chose a catalytic or unvented heater, cross-ventilate by opening a window an inch on each side of the room. It is better to let in some cold air than to run the risk of carbon monoxide poisoning.

- Do not use a gas or electric oven or surface units for heating.

- Do not burn outdoor barbecue materials such as charcoal briquettes inside, even in a fireplace.

- Do not try to use bottled gas in natural gas appliances unless you have converted the appliances for such use. Also, flues and piping made for gas-burning appliances may be unsafe for use with wood heaters.

- Have one person watch for unintentional fires whenever an alternative heat source is used. One person should also stay awake to watch for fire and make sure ventilation is adequate.

- All homes should have battery-operated smoke and CO (carbon monoxide) detectors with alarms installed.

- Keep firefighting materials on-hand.

Conserve Body Heat

- Put on extra clothing.

- If cold is severe, your bed may be the warmest place. Use extra blankets and coverings to trap body heat; this is an especially good way to keep children warm.

- Farm families might consider taking refuge in a warm livestock barn.

Find or Improvise an Alternative Heat Source

You may have alternative heating resources around your home such as:

- Fireplace, space heater, catalytic camp stove

- Wood, gas or oil heater

- Gas-fired hot water heater

Provide Fuel

Some common materials that could be used for fuel include:

- Firewood, newspapers, magazines

- Kerosene

- Woodchips, straw, corncobs

Tightly rolled newspapers and magazines can be used as paper "logs." Stack them as you would firewood to allow for air circulation. If the heating situation becomes critical, consider burning wood, including lumber and furniture.

Heat One Room

- Avoid rooms with large windows or are uninsulated - Close off all rooms except the one to be heated. When choosing a room, consider the following:

- If you're using a vented stove or space heater, select a room with a stove or chimney flue.

- Confine emergency heat to a small area.

- Choose a room on the "warm" side of the house, away from prevailing winds. walls. Interior bathrooms probably have the lowest air leakage and heat loss. Your basement may be a warm place in cold weather because the earth acts as insulation and cuts heat loss. Isolate the room from the rest of the house by keeping doors closed, hanging bedding or heavy drapes over doorways or putting up temporary partitions of cardboard or plywood.

Make sure you have a backup plan if you can't find a safe way to stay warm. Staying with relatives or going to a designated shelter might be an option.

ALTERNATIVE HEAT, LIGHT, & POWER SOURCES

FIRE STARTERS - store matches (waterproofed), butane lighters, flint & steel, charcoal starter.

FIREPLACE, OPEN FLAME (Campfire or Outside Fire Pit) suspend a Dutch oven over the heat by using a tripod, much like the early settlers did, or set the Dutch oven directly on the hot embers you have made in the fireplace or outside campfire.

WOOD BURNING - COAL STOVES use frying pans or pots on top to cook your meal.

GAS CAMP STOVES (white gas, gasoline, kerosene, propane) - Two burners using white gas will operate 4 hours on 1 quart. Use outdoors only.

BARBECUE GRILL with 5 gallon tank of propane, stores well and is easy to use.

STERNO works well for small quantities of food.

VOLCANO is a type of outdoor cook stove that you can use with 2 Dutch ovens and charcoal. It is very fuel efficient, using about half of the charcoal you would use normally with your Dutch oven. A few briquettes can roast, fry, bake, etc.

ROCKET STOVE is another type of outdoor cookstove used in many third world countries. Stoves can be constructed from brick, old tin cans, steel or be purchased. The advantage of these rocket stoves is very little fuel they need, such as wood and dry weeds, to be able to cook a whole meal.

DUTCH OVENS a 10" dutch oven with 6 or 7 briquettes on the lid and 5 or 6 underneath will cook a pot full of food. Use outdoors only.

HIBACHI - Four or five charcoal briquettes in an 8"x8" Hibachi will generate enough heat to cook a simple meal. Should only be used outdoors.

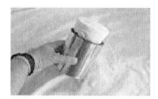

ALCOHOL STOVE – Place 1 roll of Toilet paper in 1 quart paint can – pour Isopropyl rubbing alcohol over the TP and light with a match. The can will not get hot on the bottom until the alcohol has burned down. Extinguish the flame, add more alcohol and relight. Control the intensity of the heat by adjusting the lid.

CHARCOAL STOVE – Turn a #10 Can into a charcoal stove. Cut out top and bottom of the can. Punch holes around the top and bottom. Punch many holes in the lid and wire it about half way up the can. Place the charcoal on it to light. Use a sturdy piece of wire screening, or crisscross wire across the top to create a cooking rack.

FLASHLIGHTS: New batteries last 6-7 hours of continuous use. Six-month old batteries last 5-6 hours.

CANDLES: ¾"x4" will burn 2 hrs 20 min.

COLEMAN MANTLE LANTERN: Two mantle lantern will burn 5 hours on ½ quart of white gas.

KEROSENE LANTERN: With a 1 inch wick will burn 45 hours on 1 quart of kerosene.

LIGHT STICKS are safest emergency light

GENERATORS are an excellent source of safe power. However, they use a great deal of fuel. Most run on gasoline, burning ½ to 3 gallons per hour. Itemize energy requirements in order to select the appropriate size needed. Use the smallest size possible for less fuel needs. Operate generators in an open area with good ventilation. DO NOT ATTACH the generator to your house current without approved transfer switches. The electrical "back feed" can injure or even kill utility workers repairing the power lines.

Emergency Shelter

In survival as in all aspects of life, it is easier to be organized if we prioritize. The priorities, in order, are shelter, water, heat, food, signal, and utility. You can live 4-6 weeks without food; 3-5 days without water; but hypothermia will kill you in 30 minutes. Therefore shelter is the first priority! Shelter may be defined as anything that protects the human element from nature's elements. Most importantly a good coat can't be beat, and it is easier to survive in the summer with winter clothes than in the winter with summer clothes.

What You Need

A free-standing dome or A-frame tent is the only realistic option for a mobile shelter in a short-term emergency preparedness kit. There are several things to be aware of in selecting a tent. Construction should be of good quality,  breathable materials. The rain fly should extend from the apex of the tent almost to the ground. A small rain fly like those found on many discount shelf specials is unsuitable, because it means the tent walls are made mostly of waterproof material. The human body passes 1-2 quarts of water vapor daily and if you are in a waterproof tent for an extended period of time that water vapor will condense on the walls. It is for this very reason that tube tents should be avoided.

A heavy-duty space blanket is recommended to put under the tent in order to protect the tent floor. It is much easier and cheaper to replace a $12 space blanket than a $100 tent. Avoid the pocket space blanket. Their usefulness is limited and they breed a false sense of security. A sleeping bag is the most critical piece of survival equipment you can possess, especially in winter. In a sleeping bag you can efficiently maintain body heat. A good sleeping bag will have the capability to form a hood. It will have a sizable draft tube along the length of the zipper to prevent snags. Another important feature is the ability to zip two bags together to share body heat or to put a child between parents.

Select a synthetic insulation rather than down. Qualofill, Polarguard and some of the new materials recently released are excellent. The advantage of synthetic insulation is that when the bag gets wet, it can be wrung out and will still keep you warm.

When down gets wet, the insulation value drops to nearly nothing. Emergency survival situations rarely occur on warm sunny days, and you can just about bet it will be on a dark, rainy or snowy night when the world comes apart. An absolute must in a temperate climate is a sleeping pad. Ground cold can suck the heat right out of your body, through your sleeping bag. A closed-cell foam pad will provide the insulation required, but will give little if any comfort. An air mattress of the type you take to the beach or swimming pool will freeze your whole persona during the winter. For true comfort an air mattress such as Thermarest is expensive but worth every cent. For economy, a simple 3/4-length closed cell foam pad is all that you need. Avoid open-cell pads because they soak up water just like a sponge.

In putting together a good short-term preparedness kit, you may think it necessary to initially purchase items that are of inferior quality. Perhaps so, but at the

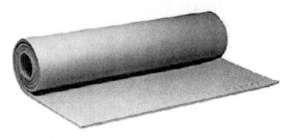

first opportunity the higher quality equipment should be purchased. There is no economy in going second class. Tents and sleeping bags are expensive and should be considered a serious investment. After all, your life and the lives of your family are in the balance!

Driving in an Emergency

Flood - *Get out of the car*

Never attempt to drive through water on a road. Water can be deeper than it appears, and levels can rise very quickly.

Most cars will float dangerously for at least a short while. A car can be buoyed by floodwaters and then swept downstream during a flood. Floodwaters also can erode roadways, and a missing section of road even a bridge-will not be visible with water running over the area. Wade through floodwater only if the water is not flowing rapidly and in water no higher knees. If a car stalls in get out quickly and move to higher ground. The floodwaters may still be rising, and the car can be swept away at any moment.

Hurricane - *Evacuate early*

Flooding can begin well before a hurricane nears land. Plan to evacuate early, and keep a full tank of gas during hurricane season. Learn the best evacuation route before a storm forms, and make arrangements with friends or relatives inland to stay with them until the storm has passed. Never attempt to drive during a hurricane or until the all clear is given after the storm. Flash flooding can occur after a hurricane has passed. Avoid driving on coastal and low-lying roads. Storm surge and hurricane-caused flooding are erratic and may occur with little or no warning.

Tornado - *Get out of the car*

A car is the least safe place to be during tornado. When a warning is issued, do not try to leave the area by car. If you are in a car, leave it and find shelter in a building. If a tornado approaches and there are no safe structures nearby, lie flat in ditch or other ground depression with your arms over your head.

Listen to radio or television for the latest National Weather Service bulletins on severe weather for the area in which you will drive.

Blizzard - *Stay in the car*

Avoid driving in severe winter storms. If you are caught in a storm and your car becomes immobilized, stay in the vehicle and await rescue. Do not attempt to walk from the car unless you can see a definite safe haven at a reasonable distance. Disorientation during blizzard conditions comes rapidly and being lost in the snow is exceedingly dangerous. Turn on the auto engine for brief periods to provide heat, but always leave a down wind window open slightly to avoid deadly carbon monoxide poisoning. Make sure the exhaust pipe is clear of snow. Exercise occasionally by clapping hands and moving around. Do not remain in one position for long, but avoid overexertion and exposure from shoveling or pushing the car. Leave the dome light on at night as a signal for rescuers. If more than one person is in the car, sleep only in shifts.

Earthquake - *Stay in the car*

Bring the car to a halt as soon as safely possible, then remain in the car until the shaking has stopped. The car's suspension system will make the car shake violently during the quake, but it is still a safe place to be. Avoid stopping near or under buildings overpasses and utility wires. When the quaking has stopped, proceed cautiously, avoiding bridges and other elevated structures which might have been damaged by the quake and could be damaged further by aftershocks.

Summer Heat - *Stay out of a parked car*

During hot weather, heat build-up in a closed or nearly closed car can occur quickly and intensely. Children and pets can die from heat stroke in a matter of minutes when left in a closed car. Never leave anyone in a parked car during periods of high summer heat.

Developing Emergency - *Stay informed*

In times of developing emergencies such as toxic material spill, nuclear plant accident, or enemy attack, keep a radio or television on and await instructions. If evacuation is recommended, move quickly but calmly, following instructions as to route to be used, evacuation shelter to be sought and other directions. If evacuation is recommended, move quickly but calmly, following instructions as to route to be used, evacuation shelter to be sought and other directions.

Dressing for the Climate You Live In

Clothing is something that is not considered often enough in planning for a disaster or in an emergency situation. Yet finding suitable clothing will be a very real concern in a disaster. You can not count on a disaster only happening on warm sunny days. Families need to be prepared to face harsh winter weather during a disaster.

The Facts

-You can only live for three hours without shelter

-Dressing properly is using the right layers and moisture management

-We loose 50% our body heat through our head at 40 degrees and 70% at 5 degrees

-Cotton Kills and Wools is warm

-A single gram of wool generates 27 calories of heat as it gets wet

-Wool retains 50% of its heat wet

-Wool absorbs 30% of its weight in water without feeling wet-cotton only 8%

-Gortex allows water vapor to exit the body but blocks water from the outside

-Cotton is designed to cool, slowly evaporating moisture held next to your body

The Dress

The best way to dress for winter weather is to wear layers. This gives you flexibility to add or remove layers, depending on the weather and your activity. In general, the three main layers are wicking, insulating and weather protection.

Wicking layer: This is the layer worn next to your skin, usually consisting of long underwear. Look for thermal underwear made of a synthetic, usually polyester, fiber that has "wicking" power. This means the fibers will wick (move) moisture away from your skin and pass it through the fabric so it will evaporate. This keeps you warm, dry and comfortable. Silk is also a good, natural fabric that has wicking abilities.

Insulating layer: This middle layer includes sweaters, sweatshirts, vests and pullovers. The purpose of this layer is to keep heat in and cold out, which is accomplished by trapping air between the fibers. Popular insulation materials include: Fleece, a synthetic material which maintains its insulating ability even when wet and spreads the moisture out so it dries quickly. Wool, which naturally wicks away moisture.

Protection layer: The exterior layer, generally a shell and pants, serves as your guard against the elements of winter. It should repel water from snow, sleet or rain and block the wind, while also letting perspiration evaporate.

Most genuine winter shells and pants are made waterproof and breathable to some extent by using tightly woven fabrics teamed with a coating or laminate. This keeps moisture on the outside but allows perspiration to escape, keeping you dry and comfortable. Depending on the weather and type of winter activity you will be doing, you may be interested in uninsulated pants and jackets/shells, or garments with increasing amounts of insulation.

Headwear: Up to 60 percent of your body's heat can escape from an uncovered head, so wearing a hat is essential when it's cold.

(Tip: If you wear a hat, you may be able to wear one less layer on your body.)

Sunglasses and goggles: Sunglasses do much more than make you look cool. They also protect your eyes from damaging solar radiation. Snow, or any other reflective surface, makes ultraviolet (UV) rays stronger, while increased altitude also magnifies the danger. On flat-light days or when it's snowing, goggles are vital. They protect your eyes and special lens colors increase the contrast so you can properly discern terrain features.

Gloves and mittens: Look for gloves and mittens that use waterproof, breathable fabrics. Mittens, in general, are warmer than gloves, but offer you less dexterity.

Socks: One pair of light-weight or medium-weight socks works best for outdoor activity. Socks are made from a variety of materials, including polyester, silk, wool and nylon. Each foot will produce 50 ml of water inactive or 200ml active. Therefore socks that have wicking properties similar to long underwear, help your feet stay dry and comfortable.

References

Sources consulted in preparation of this manual:

- www.lds.org
- www.ldsavow.com
- www.agnihotra.org
- www.aragriculture.org/
- www.ldspreparedness.com
- www.providentliving.org
- www.abysmal.com/
- The Benson Institute
- geology.utah.gov
- www.winterfeelsgood.com/

- Bozeman Stake Emergency Plan

- Principles of Self-Reliance, Silvia H. Allred, Thursday, May 1, 2008, at the BYU Women's Conference

-Personal and Family Financial Preparedness, Elder Franklin D. Richards, Ensign May 1979

-Disaster Preparation Handbook Washington Military Department Emergency Management Division

-Family Emergency Preparedness Plan Washington Military Department Emergency Management Division

-Family Emergency Preparedness Handbook

-Magna Central Stake Emergency Preparedness Manual

Other Resources of Emergency Preparedness Information:

- www.beprepared.com - (Emergency Essentials)

- www.bt.cdc.gov (CDC - Emergency Preparedness & Response)

- www.citizencorps.gov/programs/cert.shtm (Community Em. Response)

- www.disaster-resource.com (Disaster Resource Guide)

- www.fema.gov (Federal Emergency Management Agency)

- www.nws.noaa.gov (National Weather Service)

- www.neic.usgs.gov (National Earthquake Information Center

- www.nod.org/emergency/index (National Org. on Disability Em. Preparedness)

- www.providentliving.org (LDS church) - guides to food storage, preparation

- www.ready.gov (US Department of Homeland Security) much good information

- www.redcross.org/services/disaster/ (American Red Cross)

- www.training.fema.gov/emiweb/CERT/ (CERT Training)

CPSIA information can be obtained at www.ICGtesting.com
Printed in the USA
LVOW101539120612

285785LV00016B/60/P